THE DREAM BUILDERS

THE STORY OF THE FORTS OF AFRICA

Sammie Johnston

Library of Congress Cataloging-in-Publication Data

Johnston, Sammie, 1955-
  The dream builders.

  Summary: Traces the lives of Giles and Wana Ann
Fort, Southern Baptist missionaries to Africa.
  1. Fort, Giles—Juvenile literature. 2. Fort,
Wana Ann—Juvenile literature. 3. Missionaries—
Zimbabwe—Biography—Juvenile literature.
4. Missionaries—United States—Biography—Juvenile
literature. [1. Fort, Giles. 2. Fort, Wana Ann.
3. Missionaries] I. Title.
BV3625.R53J64 1989   266'.61'0922   [B]   [920] 89-8243
ISBN 0-936625-64-3

ISBN: 0-936625-64-3

New Hope
Birmingham, Alabama

N896101 ● 10M ● 0689

ACKNOWLEDGEMENTS

Jo Hesker for her help and encouragement.

Morris Johnston for his assistance in the preparation of the manuscript.

Wana Ann and Giles Fort for their time, inspiration, and sharing their life and personal mementos so freely.

This book is dedicated to Christian youth, the Dream Builders of tomorrow, two of whom are my children, Jessica and Caris.

CONTENTS

Intriguing Mission
1
Dreams Remembered
4
New Frontier
14
Dreams Realized
22
Ngangas and Chirembas
34
Christmas, Sanyati-Style
42
Peace in the Midst of Sorrow
54
More Than Medicine
62
Church Builders
76
Another Lottie Moon
82
The Four-of-a-Kind Club
90
Archie's Dream Lives On
100
Building New Dreams
106
The Dream Continues
118

PHOTO CREDITS: Pages 33, 41, 90, 126 (bottom), 127-28, FMB, Gerald Harvey. All other photographs are personal photographs, courtesy of Giles and Wana Ann Fort.

The Forts have written many articles about their missionary service for Southern Baptist publications, especially *The Commission*, the magazine of the Foreign Mission Board. Many of the stories in this book first appeared in *The Commission*.

Rhodesia became Zimbabwe in 1980.

1

INTRIGUING MISSION

*A*shrill sound rang through the still air. Wana Ann shifted in the recliner, concentration broken by the incessant ringing. She glanced lovingly at Giles peacefully napping on the couch, marked the place in her book, and rose quickly to answer the door.

"Who's there, please?"

"Special delivery for Dr. Giles and Dr. Wana Ann Fort. From Africa."

"Could it be?" pondered Wana Ann as she eagerly opened the front door. One swift glance revealed two massive boxes sitting on the front porch. "Wonderful!" she thought. The crates

1

were here at last.

"Would you please bring them in the garage?" she asked.

The two deliverymen struggled as they carried in the heavy crates. "Please sign here, Ma'am. Thank you," one said.

"Thank you. We've anxiously anticipated these for many days."

Wana Ann could scarcely contain the excitement welling up inside her as she closed the door. She quickly crossed the carpeted den floor to the sleeping man on the couch.

"Giles, dear. Wake up! Our crates have arrived."

Dr. Fort roused from his nap, slowly rubbing his eyes. "What did you say?" he asked groggily as he sat up.

"The last two crates with our belongings from Africa are here. Let's open them and check the condition of everything."

Wana Ann's excitement was contagious. Giles was caught up in the discovery of the contents of the crates, eager anticipation evident in his eyes. As they lifted each item from its resting place inside the first crate, Giles and Wana Ann joyfully reminisced about the people and events it brought to mind. They unpacked a bundle of papers, magazines, letters, and pictures.

"Oh, Giles. Seeing these papers and pictures reminds me of a telephone call I received several days ago. Suzanne Thomas called and shared that her church will soon celebrate its 35th anniversary.

"Knowing we had served in Africa for 35 years, she thought it would be interesting to compare the experiences of a missions-minded church with the experiences of a missionary couple who had begun their ministry at approximately the same time her church began its ministry. She invited us to be the guest speakers at the celebration," Wana Ann explained.

"That sounds intriguing. Is there a special emphasis at this celebration?" Giles asked.

"Suzanne said its focus will be Dreams of the Past Building the Future." She laughed.

"We surely have had our share of dreams throughout the years, haven't we?"

"Yes, we have. And God used some of them to build a medical ministry in Africa."

"You know, Giles, we still have dreams for our sons and their families. God is building some powerful ministries through them. It's exciting to dream about the witness they will have in the future," Wana Ann exclaimed.

"This celebration sounds like an excellent opportunity to share our dreams and prayers with friends. Let's get these crates unpacked!"

2

DREAMS REMEMBERED

*L*ook, Wana Ann! Do you remember this?" Giles lifted a brown, tattered scrapbook out of the crate. As her gaze settled on the frayed, yellowing pages, a soft smile settled on Wana Ann's lips. She gently took the album and caressed its worn cover with a loving touch.

"It's my remembrance book of our dates, engagement, and wedding," she warmly replied as she leafed tenderly through its pages. The pictures, programs, clipped poetry, and letters swiftly returned Wana Ann to her college years at Louisiana Polytechnic Institute (now Louisiana Tech University).

She remembered with amusement her arrival on campus. As her dad drove her up in front of the freshman girls' dorm, a young man wearing a sweater with a big *T* on the front tried to sell him a Tech license tag. Dad pulled up alongside him and, with the best country drawl he could muster, said, "I don't have any use for that. But is there any place around here where we can stop and eat these cold biscuits and bacon for lunch? I've brought my daughter here to go to college, but we need to eat these before I leave her." Dad's joking relieved the tension of the upcoming good-byes, but certainly confused that nice young man, who stood with jaw dropped as they proceeded to the dorm entrance.

However, her junior year in 1943 was the beginning of a new life adventure for Wana Ann. She faced a heavy semester course load, but still found time to participate in her beloved Baptist Student Union. As social vice-president, she planned the first BSU party of the semester, a "welcome party" for a group of transferring navy V-12 and marine students.

Little did she realize as a young sailor walked up to the registration desk that he would eventually walk right into her heart. Her dream man had always been tall, dark-haired, and slender, with gorgeous blue eyes. In reality, Giles Fort, Jr., was only slightly taller than Wana Ann, with light brown hair and brown eyes.

She realized her attraction to him as he joined her church the following day, a broad grin spreading rapidly across his face as he walked confidently down the church aisle, Bible in hand. That afternoon, at a BSU council meeting, they were paired together as prayer partners, the beginning of a partnership that never dissolved.

She later overheard a cute girl in the cafeteria naming the four boys she had "on her list." Wana Ann replied, "Well, you can just take Giles Fort off your list, because he's the only one on mine!"

"Giles, do you remember that afternoon BSU council meeting when we first discovered that we were both medical missions volunteers?"

"That was exciting and an encouragement. As a matter of fact, up until that time, I just thought you were an old brain!" Giles said.

"You know, I'd been somewhat disappointed when, as a Texas A & M junior with plans to attend medical school, I received orders from the naval V-12 program to report to Louisiana Tech for my senior year. I had never even heard of a college by that name. It was a comfort and real joy to get involved immediately in the BSU. I'd enjoyed being BSU vice-president at A & M the previous year.

"Those eight months at Louisiana Tech proved to be happy ones after all. My commitment to medical missions was strengthened and I found the wife God had prepared to share that commitment," Giles said tenderly.

"Giles, do you remember when you first made your commitment about missions to God?" Wana Ann questioned.

"It seems like it was yesterday. I was only a timid boy in junior high when I accepted Christ as my Saviour at our church revival, but I knew even then that God wanted me to do something for Him. It seems to me I always wanted to be a missionary doctor. It wasn't until my sophomore year at A & M, though, that I felt God calling me to give my life to medical missions in China. I never had a doubt about His call since that Sunday night long ago. Your call was a bit different wasn't it?" Giles asked, already knowing the answer.

"Well, I was also in junior high—in seventh grade—and it was also during our revival when I became a Christian. But I'd fought the Lord for the three previous years, trying to get up the nerve to accept Him publicly. I was also just a little stubborn." Giles smiled knowingly as she continued.

"I remember that beautiful Sunday in April. I knew what God wanted me to do that Sunday morning and they were even singing my favorite invitation hymn. But I was too stubborn to submit my will to God. Burdened with the decision I needed to make, I wrestled with the Lord in my mind most of the afternoon. Finally, I returned to the church alone and lest someone find me there, hid behind the piano. On my knees, I prayed and accepted Jesus as my Lord and Saviour. Finally at peace, I accepted Christ publicly at church that night.

"I loved Girls' Auxiliary and it was during one summer GA camp that I surrendered to full-time

8

Christian service. I was 13. I remember being a Maiden in the Forward Steps program. Miss Juliette Mather, who was then Youth Secretary of Woman's Missionary Union, SBC, gave me the pattern for the cross-stitch map of the world, one of the requirements for the Queen-with-a- Scepter step. After working like mad, I returned to camp the following summer as a Queen-with-a-Scepter; the year following I received my cape as a Queen Regent. All the work done on those steps, the studying, witnessing, mission action, fixed in my mind that God had a plan for my life.

"Before leaving for college, I sought my pastor's advice. I still was unsure exactly what God wanted me to do. Reverend Miley told me that God had blessed me with two special gifts—a keen intelligence and a great sense of spiritual sensitivity. I asked God to keep me sensitive to His voice and to His will, trusting Him to reveal His will to me. And He did.

"All spring semester of my sophomore year in college I saved money to attend Student Week at Ridgecrest Baptist Conference Center. I just knew I'd discover there that summer what God wanted me to do for Him. While there, God quietly revealed that He wanted me to be a medical missionary while I was sitting in my Sunday School class." Wana Ann paused, remembering that moment.

"I wanted to run. I went up in the mountains that afternoon. I told God all the reasons I could not be a missionary doctor. I did not have the money for medical school. The Depression had created some lean years for my family. Dad did not believe in women doctors and he certainly would not want me to be a missionary doctor. I did not want to be an old maid. And I surely did not want to study all that biology and chemistry! For three days I made excuses. Then I realized that God's love for me was great enough to demand my everything. I told God, 'All right, Lord. You will have to do it. I cannot. But now I am ready for you to bring it to pass.' "

"Here's a copy of the poem you sent me after I told you I loved you," Giles said.

"My heart still jumps a little when I think of that Sunday morning during our prayer mate meeting. I'm still not sure how I managed to teach my Intermediate girls Sunday School class after that!" Wana Ann smiled.

"You even kept souvenirs from our last date before I left for midshipman's school," he reminded her.

"That was right after our engagement. I'll never forget that bitterly cold day in February. It made me tuck my new yellow hat you'd bought me more tightly around my cold ears."

"You needed it. Your ears were always cold." He reached over and gently touched her ear. "As a matter of fact, you could use it right now!"

"The damp, chilly wind blowing through the train station mirrored the way I felt inside as we waited for the train. Plattsburgh, New York, seemed like an eternity away and I knew it would be many months before I saw you again. Before I knew it, or was ready, the train arrived and after a hug and a kiss, you were gone. I watched as you stood waving, slowly becoming a navy blue blur. Finally only wisps of dark smoke remained to indicate where your train had been. Crying, I walked several blocks to the bus station.

"Although intense loneliness and yearning were my companions throughout the months of your training and term of duty in the Pacific, I never had a doubt that our love was divinely inspired and meant to be."

Seeing a stack of letters bundled together, Giles asked, "You kept all of my letters, didn't you?"

Nodding, Wana Ann replied, "My senior year at Tech was highlighted by your letters. Those rare times you could call were treasured moments. Most precious was that week-long visit with you and your family in Fort Worth as you were on your way to amphibious training. Remember, you weren't sure you would get a leave and a few weeks before you mailed my engagement ring. See, I even put part of the wrapping in this book. My heart was really pounding when I saw you get off the train. You were certainly handsome in your uniform. Actually, you'd have looked terrific in overalls and a tattered shirt! See, here's a picture of us with your mother."

Seeing the faces of a handsome young man, a slender beauty, and a beaming mother in the picture brought a broad smile to Giles' lips. "Here's the letter telling you I'd accumulated enough points for my discharge."

"We immediately planned our wedding for June 14. I had just completed my first year of medical school at the Baylor University School of Medicine (now Baylor College of Medicine) in Houston, Texas. What excitement!" Wana Ann glowed with the happy memory.

"Here's a wedding picture, Wana Ann. You were truly beautiful in that white satin dress. It was quite a family event with my brother, David, as best man and your six sisters participating. Let's see, Marjorie was soloist; Jane, maid of honor; Polly, a bridesmaid; and even the youngest—Lee, Evelyn, and Rose were all dressed up to help at the reception. I'd always wanted a little sister and got six all at once that day!"

"It was a heavenly moment . . . a picture book day with bright blue skies and golden sunlight. The church I'd grown up in was draped in greenery, my favorite pines, and baskets of daisies. It seemed only natural that my teachers, loved ones, and friends were there," she reminisced.

"The years following that day seemed to rush by all too swiftly. They were lean, hard years financially, but happy ones. We completed our medical training at Baylor. Through our internships and residencies, God continued to confirm His call to us to serve in medical missions. Working in pediatrics until the week before our first son was born helped prepare you to serve as both a mother and a doctor in Africa."

"Yes. I remember how earnestly we prayed for

the Lord's guidance as we realized the hardships little Giles would face in pioneer missions work. I really didn't want to live where there was no electricity, no dependable water supply, no other doctor to take care of my precious baby son, no grocery store, no telephone. But I came to the place in prayer that I could tell the Lord this was impossible for me to do, but I would commit my way to Him, trusting in Him to bring it all to pass for His honor and glory. We both knew we must trust God, who gave little Giles to us, to protect him."

"The leanness of our early married years helped make money secondary in our lives. Do you remember our interview with the Foreign Mission Board as we were seeking appointment?"

Wana Ann nodded and smiled. "Yes, we were sitting sort of informally in the conference room with members of our area committee for Africa, Europe, and the Near East. They were asking all sorts of questions about our call, preparation, and beliefs. Then one said, 'The doctors I know here in Richmond live in the nicest residential areas in palatial homes. Do you two doctors realize what you will be giving up if you go to this remote area to do pioneer medical work?'

"I'll never forget that moment, Giles. You looked the questioner straight in the eye and answered, 'Sir, our Lord Jesus said that life does not consist of the abundance of the things thereof. We believe that being in His will is more important than any material goods we might ever possess.' "

"The Lord has been good to us. He has given to us abundantly of His blessings. He has led us and provided for us even more than we have needed. I'm thankful for the riches of His blessings," Giles said.

Giles and Wana Ann as a young couple.

3

NEW FRONTIER

Nineteen fifty-two was a banner year for us," recalled Wana Ann. "We became parents of Milton Giles III and were appointed missionaries by the Foreign Mission Board."

"It's easy to look back and see how God was working both in our hearts and in Rhodesia to prepare us," agreed Giles. "As we were praying about the Foreign Mission Board's request that we consider Rhodesia, missionaries in Rhodesia were praying for doctors to do pioneer medical work in Sanyati."

Wana Ann and Giles sat in silence, reflecting

back upon the events preceding their arrival in Rhodesia. Southern Baptist missions work began in Southern Rhodesia in 1950 when Clyde and Hattie Dotson were appointed. Clyde applied for and received the 100-acre mission station site in the middle of the newly opened Sanyati Reserve.

At Sanyati, the Dotsons camped out until they had built a small temporary house. They began a school and held church services under the trees in several locations. Sick people came seeking medical help, prompting Hattie to open a small dispensary.

In 1952, Ralph and Betty Bowlin moved to Sanyati from Gatooma where they had served since 1951. Betty became the first principal of the Central Primary School in Sanyati and Ralph directed the *kraal* (village) schools and evangelistic work there. The Dotsons then moved back to Gatooma.

During the rainy season in 1952, Ralph Bowlin received an urgent call for help. A young woman who lived near Neuso's *kraal* had been in labor for two days but was unable to deliver her baby. Ralph traveled in his pickup truck to her home about ten miles over slippery roads to a river too deep to cross. They waded through and brought the young woman to the truck on a stretcher held over the swollen stream. They realized they must try to get her to the nearest hospital in Gatooma so that a doctor could deliver the baby. They knew the road was very bad from all the rains, but they put some food and water in the Mission lorry (truck) and started out with her, the mother, and some men to help if the truck were stuck in mud. They did get stuck several times and were able to get out, but, finally, about 20 miles from the Mission station late this Sunday evening, the truck sank deep into the mud. Hours of back-breaking efforts failed to get the truck out and early the next morning a man was sent on a bicycle to town for help. Receiving the urgent message late on Monday, missionary Clyde Dotson managed to reach them Tuesday morning. They were camped by the side of the road, their food and water supplies exhausted. The young mother and her unborn child were dead. As Bowlin wrote, the tragedy was that she did not know Jesus. They had no way to relieve her pain or help her and she died. They dug a grave by the side of the road and buried her there. The missionary wept, "If only we had medical help she could have lived." They knelt there to pray that God would provide a hospital and send nurses and doctors to Sanyati.

"You know, Wana Ann, God uses various ways to confirm His will, but we knew immediately that we were bound for Sanyati when we heard Ralph Bowlin's recollection of his tragic experience with the mother and baby and plea for doctors. We realized the great need in that place for skilled doctors and could envision the ministry that would accompany medical work. It was exciting to receive our assignment: develop a medical program, including a hospital and outclinics, that ministered to physical needs in the name of

Christ, so that Christ might minister to man's spiritual needs."

"Yes, the assignment was exciting, Giles, but as I learned about Sanyati, I was concerned about taking Gilesie into bush country." Wana Ann thought back to the initial descriptions she read of Sanyati and Southern Rhodesia from a *National Geographic* he had purchased at a secondhand bookstore.

Much of the country was covered with low trees, shrubs, and tall grass. Along rivers and in the mountains grew tall forests. On the western border was the large Zambezi River and the majestic Victoria Falls named by David Livingstone. Wildlife was abundant: antelope, buffalo, giraffe, zebra, elephant, rhinoceros, hippopotamus, lions, leopards, and cheetahs. Several species of deadly snakes also thrived in the bush.

Though Salisbury, the capital, was a modern city with paved roads, tall new buildings, and modern conveniences, life in Sanyati bush country was far from any modern outpost.

Africans lived in primitive mud huts, with witch doctors their only source of medical help. The village was divided into ten-acre farm plots. A man's *kraal*, or home, consisted of huts for each wife, for older boys, older girls, and a cooking hut. Also there were storage huts for food during the dry season. Nearby was the cattle pen where the animals were kept at night. Men were responsible for plowing, cutting poles for the huts, weaving elephant grass thatch for roofs, constructing the huts, and discussing business. Women were occupied with mixing the mud to make plaster for the huts, as well as applying the plaster to the huts. They made pots, planted crops, later weeded and harvested them, husked corn, pounded the grain in a hollowed-out log with a pole to make cornmeal, tended the children, and cooked the family meals.

The main staple food of the Africans' diet was a cornmeal mush called *sadza*. They also ate boiled green vegetables such as cabbage and pumpkin leaves. They ate boiled dried peas, peanuts, some chicken, field mice, fish, rabbit, termites, and occasionally beef or goat meat.

Flying termites were 1½ to 2 inches long and appeared at the beginning of the rainy season. Considered a great treat, the Africans often grabbed this rich source of protein, snapped off their tails, and ate them alive. Otherwise, the termites were roasted over an open fire. Termite hills, ranging in height from 15 to 20 feet, were used to make bricks for churches and homes. Some 100,000 bricks could be made from one termite hill.

During the rainy season, which lasted from November to March, up to seven inches of rain could fall in just a few hours. The only roads leading to Sanyati were trails hacked through the bush. They became impassable during part of the rainy season. There was little opportunity to contact the outside world, since the nearest town, Gatooma, was located 60 to 70 miles away. It took four to five hours in a sturdy vehicle to travel from Gatooma to Sanyati in good weather, and all day when it rained.

"Just the thought of all those snakes made my skin crawl! Wild animals, malaria, and other tropical diseases flooded my thoughts. After all, I'd asked God to send me to a comfortable, modern city with good schools. How could I teach my own children, much less send them away to boarding school?

"I began to worry about how all these things would affect our son and any future children we might have. As I prayed, God gave me peace, an inner assurance that He would honor our commitment to His will and take care of our family. He would take care of the snakes! Still, saying good-bye to our families wasn't easy, was it?"

Giles shook his head as both reflected on those days spent packing and saying good-bye. After a pre-Christmas trip to visit with Alma Fort, Giles' mother, in Harlingen, Texas, Wana Ann and Giles packed their belongings and needed supplies in crates and big metal drums. The threesome then traveled to Wana Ann's home in Harrisonburg, Louisiana.

Little Gilesie laughed with joy at riding in the car, unaware of the aching hearts of grandparents who would be left behind. Olive Izetta Gibson waved slowly from the front porch of the home where Wana Ann was born as her precious grandson departed. David Wanamaker Gibson followed the daughter named after him to the front gate, rested his arm upon the fence post, and tipped his hat to shield his eyes from the sun.

His eyes were filled with longing as they followed his eldest daughter and her family down the road until they were out of sight. Gilesie's chubby hands patted his mother's cheeks as they headed toward New Orleans and the freighter that would take them to Cape Town, South Africa.

As they drove, Wana Ann and Giles mentally checked through the nine packed crates. Was everything there? There were tools and spare parts for the truck they would use, camera equipment, and a tremendous amount of hospital supplies and equipment. Linens and canned meat had also been packed. Of course, there were items brought especially for Gilesie: three years worth of clothing, enough shoes in various sizes to last three years, baby food, canned milk, and medicines.

Excitement mounted as the Forts joined two other missionary couples, David and Susi Lockard and Gene and Dot Kratz with 11-month old Becky, and boarded the *SS Stella Lykes*. Hearts beat rapidly as they anticipated the three-week journey across the Atlantic to Cape Town.

After arriving in Cape Town, the Forts anxiously watched longshoremen off-load their crates. Those were the reminders both of the home they had left and the new home that awaited. Suddenly, a boom slipped. Crash! One of the hospital equipment crates hit the dock. Workmen inspected the crate for damage as the Forts looked on. The stainless steel operating table was in top shape—not a single dent was visible on its shiny top. Everything was in its proper place—no damage.

At last it was time to load the power wagon and begin the road journey to Southern Rhodesia. The truck was a wonderful donation received from 20 couples in the Forts' church in Houston, Second Baptist Church. While the roads in South Africa made travel easy, the strip roads, two strips of tar on top of the gravel, encountered in Southern Rhodesia slowed the eager missionaries' journey. They made a brief stop as they crossed the Limpopo River that created the border between South Africa and Southern Rhodesia to offer prayers of praise and thanksgiving to God.

Finally, in March 1953 they reached the Dotson's house in Gatooma where they lived a few weeks with the Kratzes until they could move to Sanyati. The Dotsons were on furlough. At Sanyati, the Forts lived with the Bowlins until November when their house was built. Finally they were home!

4

DREAMS REALIZED

*U*npacking this crate reminds me of the day our crates arrived in Sanyati," mused Giles. Memories of the years spent in Sanyati and events experienced there flooded into the Forts' minds. Hours passed as they relived their ministry in Southern Rhodesia.

While waiting for the hospital to be built, the Forts worked in a crude, two-room, mud-and-pole building with a tin roof. How they watched as work progressed on the new hospital building! Already the walls were nearly roof level. One of Wana Ann's first patients was a tiny premature boy whom she had to feed with a medicine dropper. Another was a four-month-old with severe burns. Both survived.

Soon afterward, the medicine brought for Gilesie was used to treat an orderly's son who was extremely ill with dysentery. As Wana Ann knelt with the child's mother on the floor of the primitive medical building, sponging his convulsing body to lower his raging temperature, she prayed and cried along with the mother. That orderly would later become the hospital's first African director of nursing.

The missionaries at Sanyati generated their own electricity and had deep water wells. When the wells went bad, the Forts hauled nine barrels of water from the government wells located several miles away. Sometimes the generator failed, while at other times the pump malfunctioned, making the indoor plumbing useless. It certainly made for excitement!

During the first nine years of mission service at Sanyati, all the water was boiled, because there was no treatment system.

Laundry was done in a bathtub or a gasoline-motor washing machine. It was then hung outside to dry. Meticulous ironing of each item followed. The putsi fly deposited her eggs on the wet clothes as they hung drying. If they were not destroyed by ironing, maggots would hatch and burrow into the skin of the unfortunate garment wearer, causing painful boils.

The time had come to dream big dreams. African people needed training in the methods and techniques of American medicine. When the present hospital building was completed, additions would need to be made. Nurses' quarters and a nursing school were badly needed. Missionary personnel envisioned a mobile clinic system to go to the villages to do preventive medicine, child care, and prenatal work.

At long last, the 12 years of dreaming and planning culminated in a dedication program for a newly completed medical ward block, a nurses' dormitory, an aides' dormitory, an administrative block, and a pharmacy.

Giles, hospital superintendent, gave a history of the hospital. He first recalled how the hospital staff had met with an architect and engineer in 1958 to plan for the needed buildings. At that time, the hospital consisted of a single building, constructed according to a government clinic plan. Some of its rooms were equipped for obstetrical and surgical procedures, but there was no space for a central supply, X ray, a laboratory, or offices. The building plan the group devised was approved by the Baptist Mission later that year and money was gradually appropriated for the various units.

He reminded those present that 1963 was the year the first additional units were dedicated. An outpatient registration and waiting room unit, the obstetrics block, and the Cynthia Siler Morgan Memorial Chapel were completed.

The chapel memorialized a Baptist pastor's wife who requested that, in lieu of flowers at her funeral, funds be donated to the work of Sanyati Baptist Hospital. When ground was broken for the chapel, Samuel Cannata, another missionary doctor in Southern Rhodesia, preached an evangelistic sermon. He stressed that the hospital had provided medical care with an emphasis on evangelism since its beginning in 1953.

"Many people heard the gospel for the first time while at the hospital," he said. "New areas were opened to a Baptist witness because people accepted Christ as their Saviour while they or members of their families were patients at the hospital. This chapel building will make a significant contribution to the Christian witness of the hospital as it is used daily for worship services. We currently have services on the front veranda." Pastor Morgan was present for the dedication of the chapel.

The well-equipped obstetrical unit was a far cry from the wooden typewriter box that served as the first incubator at Sanyati Hospital. Portable incubators were now available, well suited to Sanyati, since they could be kept warm with hot water bottles. After all, electricity was still not available on a 24 hour basis.

The isolation building, made possible by funds from the Lottie Moon Christmas Offering, and a new loudspeaker system, a gift from Lanier Baptist Church in Baton Rouge, Louisiana, were dedicated on a May Sunday in 1965. Almost 150 people from surrounding areas attended the service, a luncheon, and an open house that followed. There were businessmen from Gatooma, and pastors, missionaries, and members of Baptist churches throughout Southern Rhodesia. It was an especially important occasion for Giles Fort because his mother was visiting. How he wished his father, Giles Fort, Sr., could have been there. He had died when Giles, Jr., was only two years old. His father had been a student at Southwestern Baptist Theological Seminary in Fort Worth, Texas, when he died.

"May all who labor here from day to day remember that they are serving the Great Physician who is able to heal sick bodies, mend broken hearts, and save sin-sick souls," said Alma Fort as she cut the ribbon to open the new building which her son had helped plan.

Wana Ann was especially happy when, in 1966, a laundry/engine room was added. Prior to that time, the 78-bed hospital laundry was done by three washerwomen who laundered all the linens, gowns, sheets, and baby clothes by hand. The clean wash was hung outside to dry, then ironed by hand with irons heated on a wood stove. A constant source of frustration existed since there was never enough clean linen to meet the needs of the hospital.

The final units were completed in 1970. As adequate facilities for inpatient care were provided, the old hospital building was remodeled to accommodate an eye clinic, an outpatient clinic, central supply, a laboratory and X ray, a pharmacy, office space, and later a dental clinic.

Giles Fort pointed out to the audience that all the money for these buildings had come from concerned Christians in the United States, given by Baptist people, often sacrificially, through the Cooperative Program and through the Lottie Moon Christmas Offering.

"The hospital as it now stands represents an accomplishment of more than 11 million Southern Baptists in more than 34,000 Baptist churches. The hospital has been built to tell the story of the love of God for all mankind, for every little baby, every boy and girl, every man and woman who may come here. Each member of the staff is also interested in telling the story of God's love."

The hospital choir then sang "I Love to Tell the Story."

Missionary Clyde J. Dotson recounted the early days of the Sanyati Mission. "After the work began at Sanyati, my wife and I lived here for a while. She helped give pills to sick people, even though she was untrained. Then we moved to Gatooma, and Ralph and Betty Bowlin came out."

Missionary Dotson then recalled the story of the young woman who died beside the road while Bowlin was trying to get her to the doctors in Gatooma. Dotson praised God for answering Ralph Bowlin's prayer for doctors at Sanyati and for continuing to answer prayers in providing medical personnel and buildings for Sanyati Baptist Hospital. He spoke of how Jesus, the Great Physician, set the example of always being concerned about the needs of people.

Two African chiefs dressed in brilliant red robes with purple trim brought greetings on behalf of the people whom the hospital served.

"I know that at one time people wondered whether I would be able to stand before them ever again," stated Chief Whozhele, one of the two chiefs in the Sanyati area. He had only recently been a patient at the hospital.

"I thank all the people who prayed to help me, the missionaries, the pastors, and people. God gave His power so that I could continue to live here on this earth. Doctors can try with everything, but without the power of God they can do nothing. I trust the doctors, but I trust God because He has the great power."

The older brother of the late Chief Neuso, who had died the previous week, represented Neuso's people. "I am thankful for what the Americans did when they came here. We let them work here. Now we are here together. We want God to help us as He did when He used His power to create the world."

Sophie Chironga, a former student at Sanyati who helped Wana Ann sew the first hospital linens and later was a hospital employee, gave her testimony. "I was born and grew up to ten years. I noticed God created me in a different way from others. My back was crooked. I became downhearted. I had no peace in my heart because there was nothing I could do for myself.

"Then two doctors named Fort came to Rhodesia. They liked me and helped me get my education.

"The bad spirit was still in my heart. In order to have rest, I wished God could have killed me. I never knew God loved me.

"One day I was crying. One of the girls saw me and took me to Dr. Giles Fort. He knew I was not sick. He said to me, 'Do you know that Christ died for you? He loves you.' Then he read Romans 8:35. From that day I was saved.

"There was no water nearby to baptize me. A vat was dug in a tall termite hill. It was lined with bricks and plastered over with cement. The men hauled water in drums. On a hot Sunday afternoon in 1953 I was 1 of 40 new believers baptized. My prayer became, 'Lord, do all what you want to do about me.'

"I knew I could never have a husband. Who would love me? But I met a fine Baptist deacon. Mr. Chironga saw me 'inside,' not 'outside.' I praised God. I never dreamed such joy could be mine.

"Both doctors prayed for me because it was difficult for me to have babies. I stayed at the hospital several months before our little girl was born. We named her Chipo which means 'gift.' We also now have a fine son."

Abel Nziramasanga, president of the Baptist Convention of Rhodesia and pastor of Harare Baptist Church, reminisced about his arrival in Sanyati in 1953 to teach at Chigovare School. He shared how his premature son, Ralph, was cared for in the mud-and-pole building used for the hospital until the first unit was built. Ralph was now a high school student.

"I express my gratitude to the Southern Baptist Convention, which has made all this possible. Baptists have sent financial help, manpower, and love that springs from Christian hearts.

"The ministry of medicine is something from God to help the people. We invite all the people to come here and be helped. The first missionaries came with the task of carrying out the commission of Jesus Christ. This is also our task as the Baptist Convention of Rhodesia. The church has the same task; we share it together."

"I have found something that is the same wherever I have gone," explained Mrs. Joan Nyathi, president of the Baptist Women's Union of Africa.

"I found it in Nigeria. I found it in Japan. I have found it everywhere Baptists do the same work as here. They seek the will of God. They worship the Lord. They seek His leadership in all their work of hospitals, schools, and churches. We receive with both our hands (only baboons take things with one hand) all the good things God gives, and thank the Lord."

Alf Revell, director of the Hospital Christian Fellowship of Rhodesia, commented to the assembled audience, "As God has answered my prayer in leading you here to organize a unit of HCF, I now pray that this will be a blessing to the ministry of the hospital. I pray that the work here may be richly blessed with souls brought to Jesus by those who love Him."

Missionary James W. Westmoreland, chairman of the Baptist Mission of Rhodesia, explained, "We of the Baptist Mission are an arm of the millions of Baptists in the United States. Because of their love, prayers, and giving, this day is possible. Because of the concern of Jesus we have built this hospital and have this ministry."

Wana Ann smiled appreciatively as she mentally compared the bleak beginnings at Sanyati Baptist Hospital with its later facilities. She remembered her first trip to Sanyati in the power wagon which served as the hospital's first ambulance. The next ambulance was an old Royal Air Force vehicle; a year later, funds were appropriated for a small Land Rover. Afterwards, the Lottie Moon Christmas Offering kept them supplied with an ambulance.

In the beginning, instruments and supplies were sterilized in Wana Ann's pressure cooker. They were then placed in the oven of her wood stove to dry. Much later a small steam sterilizer was installed, and was still serving as an auxiliary unit in the present well-equipped central supply room.

Pediatrics had its own ward now, complete with three rooms containing six to eight beds each. Lovely curtains and proper beds for infants and children furnished the rooms. This building was a dream come true for Wana Ann.

The people who came to Sanyati Baptist Hospital seeking medical help were from many places and different walks of life. Grace, a village diviner (person who tried to locate things using magical powers), came from near the Sasame station on the Gokwe reservation. This critically ill woman was greatly helped by the medical skill and loving care extended to her. One day she asked the chaplain, "How can I overcome the demons who live inside me?"

Chaplain Semwayo told her about God's power to cast out all demons and how Jesus cast out demons as He walked in Galilee.

"I want to be delivered, too," she cried.

She was delivered and made plans to burn her divining equipment upon her arrival back at home. She was anxious to return and testify about her Christian experience.

Another woman passed up several town and city hospitals to go to Sanyati for a needed operation. She recovered beautifully following surgery and was impressed by all the concern demonstrated toward her by people at the hospital. She was visited by Chaplain Semwayo, by missionaries, and by Sanyati church members. She listened to the religious services broadcast over the loudspeaker system.

Before leaving the hospital, she made a public acceptance of Jesus as her Lord and Saviour. "I know now why God let me come to this place," she explained. "My body needed help, and God gave me the help my body needed. But, most important, my soul needed help and God has given me salvation. It's wonderful! I thank God for a place that cures both body and soul!"

Information about the hospital dedication was taken from an article written by Wana Ann Fort entitled "To Tell the Story," which was printed in the March 1971 issue of *The Commission* (pp. 8-11).

Giles greets area chiefs during Sanyati's chapel dedication.

5

NGANGAS AND CHIREMBAS

*T*he superstitions, fears, and lack of education of many people in the Sanyati-Gokwe areas caused the Forts to face problems not encountered in America. Soon after they arrived in Sanyati, one of the their first patients was a young wife who had been brought many miles from her home in the Gokwe Reserve. She had been sick for several months with chronic heart failure. Her swollen body was covered with hundreds of tiny scars where the *nganga* (traditional healer) had cut it with a blade to "let out the poison" that was causing the swelling.

Although she was able to receive medicine

which gave her temporary relief, the still uncompleted hospital had no diagnostic facilities. She needed to go to the hospital in Gatooma for the long treatment her illness required. Her family wanted her cured in a week, however, so they took her home.

Another young woman was brought to Sanyati from Gokwe. She had swollen legs and remained in bed, not speaking. After several days in the hospital, she began to respond, saying, "I am sick because I stepped on the *nganga*'s medicine as I walked down a path in my village. Because of this, I can never be well. I will never sit up or walk again."

Through the kind witness and treatment she received at the hospital, however, she slowly began to improve. She was able to stand and could sit in a wheelchair. Unfortunately, some members of her family who believed strongly in the *nganga* arrived one night and wanted to take her home. "You have a bad African sickness that can never be helped by white doctors," they said.

The next morning Rhoda was much worse, lying in bed without speaking. Days passed and she improved again with the treatment of the doctors. But once again, because of her mother's and family members' insistence, she was convinced she was bewitched. She pointed to her sheets and said, "Look! Every night the poison comes out of my body. See how it stains all my sheets red."

Wana Ann explained, "Rhoda, all of our sheets have been tinted red because our borehole water has a high concentration of iron in it." Wana Ann held up other linens and pointed to the other beds in the ward. "See, the other linens are the same color of red. No poison stains them."

Wana Ann's explanations were useless. A few days later, Rhoda's relatives slipped into the hospital after midnight and carried her back to Gokwe and the power of the *nganga*.

Sickness provoked great fear in the Rhodesian people, especially when an illness lasted longer than a week. Even Christians would sometimes revert to their former superstitions.

Sunday, the Forts' house helper, began to lose weight and feel ill. Dr. Fort examined him and sent him to Gatooma for a chest X ray. Doctors there found a tumor and told Sunday he must go to Salisbury for treatment. Sunday refused.

"I will go to Gokwe to the 'Good Doctors.' The *nganga* will give me powerful medicine to get rid of the something that walks down the right side of my chest and then up the left side to my shoulder. White doctors cannot help. They only give medicine and take pictures—things that do no good."

The Forts were never able to change his mind.

The African traditional healers—*chirembas*, usually old women, and *ngangas*, men dressed in skirts of wild cat tails—carry bags of talismans and crude knives from village to village. They practice divination rituals outlawed by the government but sought by superstitious people. "Medical treatment" includes a bit of bone hung about an infant's neck, an unknown mixture caked against an abscess, cutting the body with a knife blade to create a path of escape for evil spirits, and painting the body with root dye. Many roots and herbs are also prescribed. Some medicines are poisonous if used in excess.

Early one morning a man came seeking help for his niece. Giles got in the truck and drove to the *kraal* nearest the Mission station to find the child. He brought her back to the hospital for treatment. She had tuberculous meningitis and needed to be transferred to Gatooma.

Giles and Wana Ann explained to her family, "This little girl is very sick. She has a better chance to live if she is taken to the hospital in Gatooma. There she will receive the medicine she needs. We will be happy to take her in our truck."

The little girl's mother would not make a decision. The father, as absolute head of the family, made all important decisions. The uncle found her father working in another village. Her father was extremely angry that his daughter had been taken to Sanyati and refused to allow her to be treated in Gatooma. The Forts patiently explained the severity of the girl's illness and the urgency of her receiving the necessary treatment, but to no avail.

"You may keep her with you for three days. You treat my child. If she is not well in three days, I will take her back to my *kraal*." After three days elapsed, the father returned to take his child home. She was gently placed on a stretcher and carried in the back of the truck to her little hut. As Wana Ann and Giles prayed for her before they left, people from the village gathered to watch.

Late that evening loud wailing and singing was heard in the direction of the child's *kraal*. A summons was issued for the *nganga* to come and find the cause and cure of the little girl's illness through his magic power. Several hours had passed when loud sounds of mourning were heard, announcing the death of the little girl.

Educating the African people about modern medical care was a slow but encouraging process for the Forts. It required great patience. Gradually, however, their patience and persistence paid off.

A one-year-old baby girl was brought to Sanyati Baptist Hospital. Her mother had been unable to nurse her a few months after her birth. The tiny baby slowly became very ill. Very few babies survived if their mothers died or could not nurse them since milk was either unavailable or extremely expensive. Often mothers did not know how to feed little babies and children. The little girl's mother had taken her to the *nganga* many times. Her tiny body was smeared with "medicine." Though ill, severely malnourished and anemic, she responded well to the Forts' medical treatment and was able to go home in a few weeks.

Four-month-old Peggy arrived from Gokwe after a month's illness and treatment by the *ngan-*

gas. She had a severe infection and weighed only nine pounds. Her breathing was extremely labored because her hemoglobin—normally about 11 grams—was less than 5 grams. She required several blood transfusions until her hemoglobin reached a normal level. Her family expressed their gratitude for the hospital and the life-saving treatment Peggy received.

The people gradually learned to come to the Sanyati hospital for help. A pregnant woman who had previously lost three children at birth came to have her fourth baby. She was apprehensive since, if this baby died, her marriage would be dissolved and she would be returned to her family in humiliation. She would be marked as an unwanted failure.

This kind of tribal marriage practice was the way of life for the people surrounding Sanyati. *Lobola*, or bride price, was the amount a man gave to her family for a wife. The bargain was made with the prospective bride's family; she had no voice in the matter. A first quality wife, a woman with an eighth-grade education, would require as much as ten cows. Also the groom would buy clothing and blankets for her mother and others. Cows were a valuable commodity. They were rarely slaughtered for meat because they indicated the extent of a man's wealth. A prospective husband's family might work for years to accumulate the wealth needed to acquire such a wife. Wealthy men were able to have more than one wife. Although most could afford only one, polygamy was common.

The marital agreement hinged on the wife pro-
ducing living children. If she didn't, the husband
had the right to return her to her family and have
his *lobola* refunded. A single stillbirth was enough
to end a marriage.

Giles realized how unusual this woman's husband was to give her so many chances. He prayed
as he prepared to perform the cesarean section in
the gleaming surgery of Sanyati Baptist Hospital.
He was thankful for her husband's patience, for
his own training and preparation. Moments later,
the gusty, healthy cries of a newborn baby were
heard. The mother began to ask in a voice filled
with joy and ecstasy that could only come from
one who had lost three previous babies in child-
birth, *"Mwana wangu! Mwana wangu, here?
Mwana wangu mupenyu!"* (My child, is this my
child? My child is living!). She accepted Christ
as her Lord and Saviour as she was recovering in
the hospital.

An uncle arrived early one morning to seek
Wana Ann's help for his nephew. The boy had
suffered through the previous night with a high
fever and convulsions. Upon examining him,
Wana Ann realized he was critically ill with encephalitis. As the day wore on, it became obvious
the unconscious child would not live. Feeling the
heartache of the boy's mother, Wana Ann explained to her that only God could intervene to
spare the little boy's life.

His mother's face reflected a quiet serenity as

she spoke in broken, halting English. "Doctor, do not worry. Is no matter now. God gave boy. We happy. He was good boy. Now God take boy. That will of God. Is all right now. No worry."

Humbled by the quiet Christian faith of the mother, Wana Ann marveled as she sat with her, watching his life slip away. Once again she was reminded that Christ was the answer to the needs of this sick world. How thankful she was that God had given her and Giles this place of service in His kingdom.

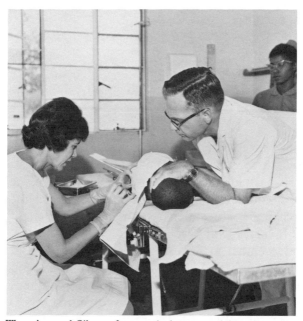

Wana Ann and Giles perform a spinal tap on a child at Sanyati.

6

CHRISTMAS, SANYATI-STYLE

*D*o you remember this?" Giles asked Wana Ann, holding up a faded red Christmas stocking he had pulled from a crate. "How could I forget Christmas in Sanyati?" Wana Ann countered. She smiled as she fingered the stocking bearing their son's name, and thought of holidays long past.

December in Sanyati was very different from the Decembers Wana Ann spent in Louisiana and Texas. It was the hot, rainy season in Southern Rhodesia and people were busy planting crops. The rainy season lasted from November to March. The farmers depended on the crops planted during the rainy season to sustain their families through the dry season, April through October.

The Bowlins were on furlough in the United States and Giles was away from the station a great deal of the time. Wana Ann kept busy with cooking, housework, tending the dispensary, and taking care of Gilesie. Between typing the minutes from the August Mission meeting and writing the annual report for Southern Rhodesia to the Foreign Mission Board, she wrote Christmas letters to friends and family. She was anxious to get those new floral curtains finished and hung in the living room in time for Christmas. They had been in their house just a few weeks.

The Sunday before Christmas arrived. Wana Ann took all of her Nativity scene figures for her children's Sunday School class to see. How excited the 25 children were as they touched the brightly colored shapes while Wana Ann told them the Christmas story! Giles took cards containing the Christmas story to the children in each of his Sunday School classes in five different villages, where he preached every Sunday.

Delight shone from everyone's face as Giles returned from Sunday services with a Christmas tree. It didn't matter one bit that it was not a traditional evergreen Christmas tree, but a tree native to Africa. In fact, it was just a thorn bush! After dinner, the schoolchildren came and helped decorate the tree. They were almost as excited over the sparkling, colored lights, the first they'd ever seen, as was Gilesie. How thankful they were that Giles' mother, Alma, had given them the lights and beautiful ornaments. Gilesie got so caught up in the Christmas spirit that it was ten o'clock before he fell asleep!

The next day found Wana Ann busy with preparations for the Tuesday Mission meeting. Sanyati was in bloom and fresh flowers filled the house: red zinnias and salvia in a white bowl in the living room, petunias in the bedrooms, and a bowl of greenery accompanied by Christmas balls on the dining room buffet. The air was filled with the delicious aroma of an applesauce cake cooking in the wood stove oven. A commotion in the driveway outside sent Wana Ann scurrying to determine its cause.

There sat a new ambulance! Missionary David Lockard sat smiling behind the steering wheel of the vehicle he had purchased at the Royal Air Force base auction. Southern Rhodesia RAF bases were closing down, so equipment was available at an excellent price. This field ambulance was old, but it had four-wheel drive, a searchlight, and a siren. Wana Ann spied the right-hand steering wheel and made a mental note that Giles would need to give her a driving lesson in it! This surprise and the package that arrived from a friend named Willadene containing a gorgeous red felt stocking with Gilesie's name on it brightened the Fort household's Christmas spirit.

Mission meetings on Tuesday and Wednesday kept everyone occupied. Planning at Mission meetings was always accompanied by a lot of

prayer. Missionaries realized their stewardship responsibilities and trusted in the Lord's timing to
meet their needs. The hospital team decided what
to recommend. They considered the overall hospital development, listed the needs, and decided
where to place each one on the list of priorities.
Funds for equipment, full-term missionaries, and
volunteer workers were all considered.

These were presented to the general Mission
meeting and all of the missionaries voted on which
of these needs to recommend. The requests were
then sent to the Foreign Mission Board. Over a
year would pass between the time requests were
made and when the Mission station would receive
a response.

Wana Ann wondered what little face would
brighten next year's Christmas celebration as she
donned a maternity dress. Everyone on the Mission station would be at the Fort home that evening to listen to their recording of the *Messiah*.
Later, they would wrap Christmas packages with
the elegant paper sent by Giles's mother.

Christmas Eve arrived at last. Wana Ann rose
early and began making preparations for the afternoon and evening parties. She baked a white cake
in the Christmas tree pans her mom had sent,
concerned about how its baking would be affected
by the wood stove. She delighted in the stunning
results, especially after its completion with the
pale green icing, nuts, dates, and cherries. Next
she set about making Christmas tree cookies using
the cookie press. She chose bits of pineapple and

cherry to create ornaments on the "trees." So irresistible they begged a taste test, she obliged. Yum!

Hattie Dotson and Susi Lockard came over to assist with preparations for the evening party. Discussing events of the past week made time pass quickly as they made tuna and pimiento cheese sandwiches; stuffed dates with fondant, rolling them in powdered sugar; and made small pieces of candy topped with pecan halves. Most of the ingredients for these goodies came in Christmas boxes from the US. Preparations completed, they dashed to the hospital just in time for the workers' party.

Seventy people, including 40 children, were present. It was quite an event with everyone fancifully dressed. Everything looked festive draped in bright crepe paper. The children were thrilled with their toys. The girls received reconditioned dolls, while the boys played gleefully with their blocks, cars, and tops. The men received clean, pressed ties; the women were presented with aprons. Everyone especially enjoyed the punch and cookies. Mufundisi Sithole, an African minister, read the Christmas story from Luke and everyone joined in singing several Christmas songs in the Shona language.

After the hospital party, Wana Ann hurried home to finalize preparations for the evening Mission party. She immediately tackled the task of decorating the dining room. The table held the lazy Susan, the center of which was arranged with

red and green candles, greenery, plastic snow-
men, and Christmas balls. White candles and
Christmas balls surrounded the outer compart-
ments which were then filled with mint balls,
dates, and colored fondant candies. Silver candle-
holders containing tall green candles flanked the
sides.

The Christmas tree cake, crystal salad plates,
forks, and Christmas napkins filled one end of
the table. Plates of open-faced sandwiches cut in
star, tree, and circle shapes; cookies; mints
straight from Dallas, Texas; bonbon dishes of
cashew nuts and peanuts from Louisiana, and a
tray with crystal glasses of punch filled the other
end of the table. The fruit punch was delectable
with red and green cherries, mint leaves, and
orange and lemon slices floating in the ice.

The party was delightful! Everyone enjoyed the
tree, food, and listening to music. Playing cha-
rades was such fun. Everyone received a paper
hat and crackers that Susi brought from Bulawayo. These crackers were from England, made
of rolled crepe paper and decorated. When pulled
from each end, there was a loud 'pop'. Inside
were little toys and a paper with a fortune written
on it. What fun! Gifts were exchanged and Gilesie
liked that idea so much that he wanted to open
everyone's present.

Christmas Day 1953 brought a deep blue sky
flecked with fleecy clouds and bright sunshine.
Gilesie awakened a bit after seven calling,
"Daddy, Daddy." Giles brought him to their bed

while Wana Ann pretended to be asleep.

Gilesie crawled up to her head, patted her cheek, and opened her eyes with his fingers until she greeted him. He then put his head on the pillow, closed his eyes, and had a smug little grin as Wana Ann said, "Oh, just look at that little boy with his head on the pillow, so tired. Pat him, Nani (Gilesie's name for her) and Daddy." After playing a few minutes, she said, "Gilesie, let's go see what Santa left under the Christmas tree for you."

Immediately he darted down the hall and stopped abruptly in front of the red wheelbarrow sitting under the tree. What joy radiated in his eyes and in his smile as he tried it out! A bit later, he was persuaded to open his gaily wrapped gifts: a pull-toy bear playing a xylophone, several books, a big truck, and a Baylor dog. The stuffed dog's ears fascinated him so much that he would pull its ears, then run to his real-life dog, Dixie, and pull on her ears, all accompanied by his cries of "ear, ear." Patient, loving Dixie seemed to understand his excitement and took all the ear pulling quite good-naturedly.

Spying his stocking, Gilesie emptied it in short order, finding small cars, candy, cookies, an orange, and an apple (a tiny thing saved expressly for the stocking). He remained nicely entertained with his loot while Nani cooked breakfast. The Bowlins then added to his exhilaration with a set of play garden tools. He promptly began a dirt transfer project in the backyard, aided, of course, by his shiny red wheelbarrow.

Missionaries began to gather at ten for the morning program. How exciting to find all the Southern Rhodesia Baptist missionaries in attendance! A few African people were present; on the roads and trails to the station, more could be seen as they walked along, smiling and chatting, in their usual unhurried stroll. Many came on bicycles, others on the backs of lorries (trucks).

By eleven a large crowd had gathered on the front veranda of the hospital and the service began. Everyone—missionaries, station workers, and people from the reserve—had come to hold the opening service for the new Baptist Hospital.

In his sermon that morning, Clyde Dotson reviewed the steps that had brought everyone to that moment. Southern Baptist work began in Rhodesia in 1950 when the Dotsons were appointed as missionaries. The government had created the Sanyati Reserve and begun to move large numbers of African people into the area. Government policy was to grant one missions group a central station in each reserve. Only this station was allowed to have resident missionaries. Mr. Dotson applied for the station at Sanyati and it was granted to Southern Baptists.

The Dotsons, including three-year-old Dorothy Joy, moved to Sanyati to begin work on the reserve. The area was unoccupied except for lions, leopards, hyenas, wild dogs, elephants, baboons and monkeys. The elephant path leading to the river ran directly across the station.

The Dotsons lived in a small mud-and-pole building. Mrs. Dotson set up a dispensary in a two-room, mud-and-pole building to supply as much treatment as possible to the people who begged for medical help. How grateful she was when Edith, an African nursing orderly, was employed, since Mrs. Dotson was untrained in medicine.

After relating the story of the young woman Ralph Bowlin tried to take to Gatooma for help, Mr. Dotson exclaimed, "Thank God, Southern Baptists care!" Money from Cooperative Program funds came and in 1952 the building program for the hospital began. Plans were obtained from the government and African labor was used to build the hospital. The Foreign Mission Board appointed hospital personnel. Monda Marler, a nurse, arrived in December 1952, and directed the dispensary. Dorothy Kratz, a laboratory technician, arrived in March 1953, along with the Forts.

Building the hospital so far from a town caused many hindrances; the African people were not fast workers. Patients were seen in the old dispensary, with beds set up in one room and in a nearby storage shed. During a severe flu epidemic, 30 patients were scattered around the station in a multitude of windy rooms and huts. In spite of all the inconveniences, many lives and souls were saved. Crates of hospital equipment arriving from America were an encouragement that the hospital would soon be completed.

As Mr. Dotson completed his review of the brief history of medical work at Sanyati, he called upon those gathered to thank God for answering the prayers of the people; for providing the building, workers, and equipment. Hearing this exhortation caused Wana Ann to realize that God was using her skills and willingness to serve Him to answer prayers, just as He was using Southern Baptists back home who gave financially to answer prayers. She thought of the words of Paul in Romans 10:14, "How shall they hear without a preacher? And how shall they preach, except they be sent?" (KJV). God added a blessing at the close of the service as two young girls became Christians.

Wana Ann reflected upon the gifts she had received and those the people of Sanyati Reserve had received through the hospital ministry; she marveled at the dreams He had given them to dream for the future ministry of the hospital. The hospital had 40 beds with three wards, one each for men, women, and children. A small room used for labor was sometimes also used to house mothers and babies when the small room for them overflowed.

No isolation facilities forced the doctors to use the warehouse to isolate diphtheria, meningitis, and other communicable diseases. The outpatient department was extremely small and there was no waiting room.

With funds provided through the 1954 Lottie Moon Christmas Offering, the staff hoped to provide a waiting room, isolation ward, and family quarters. Some member of each patient's family usually stayed to help care and cook for him or her. They frequently slept on the floor by the patient and cooked under a big tree in back of the hospital. Cooking was tough during the rainy season!

Hospital employees lived in various inadequate buildings around the station. There was one residence for a married couple, with two more under construction. Within a few years, a nursing school would be established, solving the need for African workers.

Another nurse was desperately needed. When the hospital staff was freed of other station responsibilities, they planned to establish outpatient clinics throughout the reserve. Presently, people seeking medical treatment often walked or bicycled more than 15 miles each way.

Compared to hospitals in America, Wana Ann knew Sanyati Baptist Hospital was not very fine. But compared to African hospitals in Rhodesia, it was very good, with the equipment as adequate as anything found elsewhere in the country. Africans still asked if Europeans were moving to Sanyati. They could not believe such a hospital was being built for Africans!

Most important, however, was the spiritual work of the hospital. Mufundisi Sithole held chapel each day. It was attended by both outpatients and inpatients able to get out of bed. He visited others at their bedsides. Missionaries visited and witnessed to the patients, with one visiting each ward daily for prayer before breakfast. Several hospital employees spoke to patients about the Christ who loved them and could heal their sin-sick souls.

Pioneer work in an isolated area often brought unique problems. Sometimes people wondered why Wana Ann and Giles were happy to serve God there. An engineer from a mine who came to check the Mission station diesel engine asked, "What did Dr. Fort do back in America that made it necessary for him to leave and come to a remote place like this and do the kind of work he is doing?"

A Christian from Gatooma accompanying him replied, "If the Lord Jesus loved sinful man enough to die for him, is it so strange that man should love the Lord Jesus enough to leave home gladly to serve Him, even here?"

7

PEACE IN THE MIDST OF SORROW

*A*s Giles and Wana Ann continued to sort through their possessions, they were carried forward in time from their happy first Christmas to a sad memory of the loss of a close friend, and to many other memories of life at Sanyati.

The Forts met Headman Mudzimba at Mudzimba Kraal when they first came to Sanyati. For almost 20 years, he and Giles enjoyed a good friendship. Whenever Giles shared with him his need for Christ, however, he would always refuse, saying he would wait awhile. He became ill with heart problems in 1972 and was admitted to Sanyati Baptist Hospital. As chaplain Mufundisi Semwayo visited and prayed with Baba (Mister or Father) Mudzimba in his room, Giles' prayers for Baba Mudzimba's salvation were answered— he accepted Jesus as his Saviour. Responding well to medication, he soon returned home and continued his work.

In September of that year a message came to the pastor at Sanyati that Baba Mudzimba was ill and wanted to see him. Mufundisis Muchechetere and his wife immediately went to Mudzimba's village. Upon finding the old man extremely weak, Mufundisis Muchechetere insisted they call the ambulance. Baba Mudzimba refused, saying it was time for him to die and he was ready. He asked the pastor to pray for him, then expressed his gratitude and assured his visitors he was ready to be with Jesus.

He died the following evening. The Forts went to the funeral, taking with them the burial box made by the station carpenter and covered in cloth by the Woman's Missionary Union women. A great number of people were present, for Baba Mudzimba was an important man in the area.

Many of his family members were not Christians and followed the traditional Shona customs of mourning. Women sat on the floor of a hut with the body and greeted visitors, while the men sat outside. In spite of that, the funeral service was evangelistic. Hymns were sung as the simple wooden box was carried out of the village to the top of the termite hill near the cattle pen. Pastor

Muchechetere preached an evangelistic message, inviting all present to follow Baba Mudzimba's example and accept Jesus as Saviour. A prayer of gratitude for his life and acceptance of Christ followed, with a prayer of intercession for unsaved tribal members concluding the service.

As the crowd departed, each woman dropped a kernel of corn in a small basket. Each man dropped a kernel in another basket. Afterward, someone counted the kernels to calculate attendance, as was the custom.

Walking slowly back to the Land Rover, the Forts thanked God for saving the soul of an old friend while he was in the hospital. They also prayed for the people with whom they'd sat on the dusty hillside who still did not know Jesus.

One day late in November a father came to the hospital from the distant Gorodema village in Gokwe Reserve. He brought along a tiny, undernourished, four-pound baby. He related how his young wife had had a complicated delivery and the old *ambuyas* (grandmothers) were unable to help. After the baby was born, the young mother died on the mud floor of the African hut.

The *ambuyas* attempted to care for and feed the baby with a thin porridge of boiled cornmeal. As the father watched the baby grow thinner and weaker as the days passed, he decided to take him to the Baptist Hospital, hoping that his life might be saved. Though given intravenous fluids and fed with a dropper at the hospital, weakness and infection snuffed out the spark of life in the little boy.

As soon as word reached the baby's father, he made the long journey to the hospital. Frances Greenway, missionary doctor, counseled with him when he arrived. She spoke with him about his baby, assuring him that the little boy had gone to be with Jesus. She shared how much Jesus loved and cared for him. As he left the hospital to find a place to sleep, she placed some gospel tracts written in his own language in his hand.

The following morning Lucy, a young Baptist woman who worked for Greenway, came with nourishing food she had cooked for the weary father. Baba Mahole and other hospital workers volunteered to go with the father and help him dig a grave. African custom dictated that the baby be buried near a *vlei* or swamp area. The men went there to dig the grave and then returned to their huts in their village. The women accompanied the body to its burial.

Mai (Mrs. or mother) Muzenhenhamo and other women from the hospital sang Christian hymns as they went to bury the baby. Pastor Magaramombe spoke words of comfort to the father, read God's Word, and prayed, telling the man how he might be saved. The pastor returned from the funeral, joy radiating from his face.

"It was easy to lead this man to accept Jesus as his Saviour. His heart was prepared and ready. He had attended some of the services held at

Gorodema by the African ambulance driver Machona. He showed me the tracts Dr. Greenway gave him last night. Someone in the hospital compound had read them to him. He accepted Jesus as his Saviour."

As the father prepared to return to his village, he asked for another tract containing the plan of salvation. He wanted it for his brother. Many in Sanyati were laborers together so that this young father might know Jesus and share Christ with others.

May is a beautiful month in Sanyati. The vegetation is lush and green from the abundant rains and the weather is delightfully cool. People smile and sing as they harvest crops of corn and cotton. Such beauty was the backdrop for a young father's anguished cry, "Clifford is dead. My son, my only son, is dead. Do not fear my son, for I shall follow you one day."

He then began to pray, thanking the Lord for the precious son who had lived in his home for only three short months. He beseeched the Lord to comfort broken hearts and give him an opportunity to witness of God's sufficient grace in his time of sorrow.

For several days, the Forts had worked with and prayed for the life of this little boy. The encephalitis that attacked his brain had advanced until recovery was impossible unless God chose to perform a miracle.

As the Forts gathered under the trees by the

vlei, they listened to the message of hope through faith in Jesus Christ and shared in a time of prayer for strength and courage in the midst of sorrow, and for zeal to share Jesus with those who lacked that strength. As they watched the gentle breeze blow lightly across purple water lilies and majestic birds swoop down from the deep blue heights, they realized little Clifford's death had been a witness to many, enabling his parents to be powerful witnesses through their deep, abiding faith to their people.

The first twins in the little mud-and-pole dispensary building where the Forts' medical work in Sanyati began were Peter and Paul, sons of the Chivangas' oldest daughter. Through the ensuing years, Ambuya Chivanga, Peter and Paul's grandmother, came to know and love Jesus, but Baba Chivanga continued his love affair with liquor. Then tragedy struck. Peter was knifed and killed by an angry man.

Baba Chivanga was ill and unable to attend Peter's funeral. He had become a Christian, however, just prior to Peter's death. He sent a relative to deliver his message at the funeral. He had refused to follow Jesus for many years. Since he had repented, he had thrown out the drink and was obeying the Lord. He urged all the family and friends present to trust Christ as Saviour. He expressed his deep sorrow over Peter's death, but was glad that Peter had been a Christian, a good boy, a hard worker, and obedient to his mother.

Now he was with Jesus.

He extolled a warning that everyone faced death, perhaps coming unexpectedly like Peter. Everyone needed to be prepared by obeying Jesus now. He himself had peace in his heart because of his love for his Lord.

The women in WMU went later to pray with the grieving family. Peter's grandmother, Ambuya Chivanga said, "My mother died when I was very young and I often had little to eat. I always saved part of my food to share with my younger sister. I learned early in life that Jesus loves orphans. God gave me a good husband, a happy life, and a good family. As our children grew, they became Christians, all except Peter's mother, our oldest daughter."

The firstborn is very important in a Shona family and the love flowed from the old woman's eyes to Peter's mother who, seated with the other women, was dressed in the traditional black mourning dress and head scarf.

"I prayed many years and my heart ached inside because this daughter was rebellious against the Lord." Tears glistened in her eyes.

"This past year, this my beloved firstborn repented and trusted Jesus. We then began to pray for her husband who just recently accepted Jesus. Now in their time of deep sorrow, they have peace in Christ."

Soon afterward, Peter's grandfather, Baba Chivanga, was examined at Sanyati Baptist Hospital. A malignancy was discovered. He left the hospital, choosing to spend his last days at his home. The Sunday before he died he told his family, "I am ready. My only regret is that our church is not yet built. Take this money for an offering and see that there are chairs in the church when it is built."

After his death, great numbers of people visited the family. When a woman began the customary mourning, Ambuya Chivanga reminded them that Baba said he would not rest properly if people shed tears. He was happy with the Lord and wanted the people to sing hymns. His wife, a rock of strength to her family, began, with others joining in, singing hymns to glorify her Lord!

8

MORE THAN MEDICINE

*I*n the women's ward of the Sanyati Baptist Hospital were two *ambuyas*, one more than 80 years old, who had accepted Christ as their Saviour. The older woman had lived more than 80 years in fear and superstition with no knowledge of God or His Son, Jesus. She had never gone to a church service, never heard a preacher or listened to the reading of God's Word. But when she became ill with pneumonia and traveled with her family to receive medical treatment at the hospital, she received far more than a healed lung.

She shared, "For a long time I have worshiped

many different things because I did not know what I should worship. Today in the hospital I heard of the one God and His Son, Jesus, and now I know whom I should worship. I want to follow Jesus."

A missionary visited in the home of a very sick man. Both he and his family knew he was dying and saw no reason for him to be hospitalized. Knowing the sick man was not a Christian, Dr. Fort insisted he come to the hospital.

He improved with the medical treatment he received at the hospital. Many people prayed for him and talked with him about becoming a Christian. For more than two weeks, he refused to accept Jesus. After the worship service one Sunday morning, Dr. Fort and a schoolboy visited with him. As they turned to leave his ward at the end of their visit, the man called them back to say he wanted to accept Jesus as his Saviour. Later that week he died. What a difference coming to the Sanyati Baptist Hospital made in his life and death!

The rainmaker at Maponi Line, the village nearest the Sanyati Mission station, was greatly feared and respected. She occasionally brought her children to the hospital for treatment, but steadfastly refused to allow them to be hospitalized. Her youngest child became critically ill with pneumonia, and after traditional remedies failed to help him, she brought him to the hospital.

Her fear that her child would die overcame her

fear of staying at the hospital. The red hospital blankets frightened her; at night, she covered her son's red blanket with the big black cloth that signified her position and had served as his blanket all of his life. She herself would not sleep inside the hospital.

How Wana Ann prayed that this child would recover! Each time she gave him medicine, she told his mother that she was praying for him and trusting in God to help him recover.

He soon began to get better and was able to return home. Wana Ann was thankful for this powerful witness to the people at Maponi Line. A large number of his relatives soon came across the river for medical care. Wana Ann knew they would never have walked the many miles to reach the Sanyati Baptist Church, but because they came to the hospital, they heard the good news of Jesus who died for them.

Wana Ann was always happy when she could help make sick people well and was grateful for her medical training and the available facilities to treat disease, diagnose illness, and relieve pain and suffering. But her inner joy of gratitude came from the daily opportunities presented through the hospital to tell lost people about Jesus. How her heart rejoiced when patients accepted Christ as Saviour!

The first pair of eyeglasses fitted in the eye clinic at Sanyati Baptist Hospital enabled a teacher at a Baptist school to perform his classroom duties.

Teacher Muvindi held one hand over his right eye and said in a concerned voice, "My eye is very painful and I cannot see well with it." He had traveled ten miles to Sanyati Baptist Hospital from Kasirisiri Kraal School where he lived and taught.

Giles was grateful for the well-equipped eye clinic at the hospital and for his training in ophthalmology. He had previously experienced tremendous frustration as he saw numerous cases of acute and chronic eye disease but was unable to treat them. He used his second furlough to take the necessary residency training in ophthalmology. He carefully examined Muvindi's eye and transferred him to the city hospital where an eye specialist could provide emergency treatment and preserve his eyesight.

Two weeks later, Muvindi returned to Sanyati Hospital for continued treatment. His vision spared, complete healing would require constant treatment over an extended period of time. At last, Giles fitted the teacher with glasses. Muvindi was elated that he could read again and continue to teach.

The arrival of summer missionaries in Sanyati was preceded by a great deal of planning. In three Southern states, college students on many campuses planned and worked to collect the money necessary to support the Baptist Student Union summer missionary project for Sanyati. Students completed applications; committees met to interview, pray about, and choose those who would go. Finally, four students were selected.

At Sanyati, the Forts and other missionaries met to pray and plan. Knowing the cost to send the young people, they planned the best ways to utilize the talents and training of the four students for the two months they would be at Sanyati.

When the BSU summer missionaries arrived, they were warmly welcomed and put right to work! Their youthful vigor, contagious enthusiasm, and spiritual concern were a much-needed "shot of vitamins" to the Sanyati missionaries.

The students made significant professional contributions. Carolyn Roberson, a registered nurse from Texas, assumed a position of responsibility working with the hospital staff and in the well baby clinic. Betty Roebuck, a South Carolina pharmacy major, began to organize the drug room. Van Williams, a Mississippi medical student, made rounds in the wards and clinics and helped in obstetrics and surgery. His wife, Sarah, directed the hospital choir, played the piano for chapel services, and did a huge amount of typing and mimeographing for the hospital.

The students served in many ways. They went into the villages on Sunday to worship, visit in homes, preach, and teach. They helped cook for special dinners, entertained guests in their apartments, baby-sat, taught an MK (missionaries' kid) while the mother was away, and sewed. The Africans expressed love for them and thanked God for their coming.

As they prepared to leave Africa the missionaries reflected on their time there. "As I return to my university," commented Betty, "I shall be more aware of international students, since I now know what it is like to be a stranger in a foreign land. I hope to welcome and befriend them as I was received in Rhodesia."

"I have seen that life on the missions field is very much like life in the US," concluded Carolyn, "with the same temptations, joys, difficulties, discouragements, and the same supreme goal— to lead others to a saving knowledge of Jesus Christ."

Van observed, "I was made aware of the tremendous opportunity to spread the gospel during the chapel services in the hospital, when many heard the gospel who would not have attended a preaching service under different circumstances. I was impressed with the laymen who worked in the hospital and were eager to preach and witness. After having worked here and seen missions in this country, my view of missions and my call to missions have been more solidified."

Some years later Carolyn Roberson served as a missionary in Zimbabwe and Bophuthatswana. Van and Sarah Williams were missionaries to India for several terms.

The sign on the door read "Joe's Place," but the door didn't open into a hamburger stand or tavern. It was the dental clinic at Sanyati Baptist Hospital.

"Joe" was Joseph Pipkin, a dentist with a private practice in Orlando, Florida. A Baptist layman, he decided to get directly involved in world missions by giving a personal Christian witness through his professional training.

Little dental care was available for most Africans in Southern Rhodesia because its cost was completely out of the range of the majority of incomes, and the nearest dentist was very far away. When outpatient work began at Sanyati Baptist Hospital, patients with throbbing toothaches and painful gums came to receive treatment; since equipment was meager with no light or chair, and knowledge of procedures was sparse, about all that could be done was extract the tooth.

The news that a dentist was coming to Sanyati Baptist Hospital, if only for two months, was welcome news to the Forts. He was even bringing his own equipment and an assistant!

On their first full day in Rhodesia, the Pipkins met several African dentists and visited the government mobile dental clinic before heading to the Sanyati bush country. After a day of rest and orientation at the Fort home, they went to work. Their equipment had arrived earlier and was already installed, ready for use. Since advance arrangements for treatment had been made for pastors and their families, hospital staff, teachers and students, and church leaders, the Pipkins stayed busy from 8 A.M. until 10 P.M., pausing only for meals.

After the Pipkins left, the effects of their work

continued. Mai Chikoo, an ample and jolly pastor's wife, once again flashed a broad smile. One by one her teeth had been extracted due to tooth decay. Because they had a large family and a small income, their budget allowed no remedy for treating teeth except removal when the pain became unbearable. She had been one of the first patients at "Joe's Place." She and her husband managed to scrape together the train fare to Gatooma and the cost of the bus ride to Sanyati Baptist Hospital, the place with the *Chiremba wezino* (doctor of teeth). Pipkin prepared dentures for her.

Mai Chikoo was ecstatic as she prepared to attend the annual WMU Convention, where she served on the registration committee. As she flashed her winning smile, the women exclaimed, "Ah, Mai Chikoo. You have been made just like a young girl again!" There was much singing and clapping as the women celebrated with her.

Wana Ann and Giles stood on the veranda and smiled in gratitude as they surveyed the hospital compound, remembering all the missionaries, summer student missionaries, and lay volunteers who had participated in the medical ministry. How they praised God for the skilled hands of surgeon Maurice Randall; for full-time dentist John Monroe; for pharmacist and business manager Ed Moses; nurses Helen Roller, Guy Lockmart, Mary Clark, Carolyn Roberson; midwifery school director Margaret Dunaway; lab technologist Terri Sutley; clinic doctors Bob Garrett and

Sam Cannata; and Sanyati Baptist Hospital doctor Frances Greenway.

The hospital served an area populated with approximately 300,000 people. Because many of these people often had to walk two or three days to reach the hospital, a mobile clinic program began to take the hospital facilities to the people. The clinic program reached into the surrounding areas of Gokwe and Sasame, and a number of clinics were built along with homes for staff nurse orderlies. New staffers and extensive training for the old ones resulted in many new services at the hospital: ophthalmology, dentistry, nutrition training, midwifery school, and a pharmacy. Still, medical evangelism remained the primary goal.

Thinking of the clinics brought an unnerving experience vividly to mind. Giles was on a trip to the clinic at Gokwe. His Missionary Aviation Fellowship (MAF) plane was scheduled to return early one afternoon but did not. Radio contact was lost. Government officials eventually set out in a Land Rover seeking signs of wreckage.

They found the crashed plane the next morning about 12:30 A.M. A field of millet had caught the wheels of the plane and flipped it over as it attempted to gain altitude off the wet field. Giles, the pilot, and an African orderly were found unharmed, suffering only from mosquito bites, hunger, and exposure.

While waiting to be rescued, Giles reexamined his call from God. He was cold, hungry, and miserable from the swarms of mosquitoes pestering him. He knew that the medical help he had given earlier that day was only temporary. The medicines and cures were not permanent. But he had had an opportunity that day to share God's love and salvation, and that was permanent. He was still where God wanted him.

Little Washington was brought to the hospital with pertussis encephalitis and severe pneumonia. Gasping for breath, he convinced the nurses several times that he was dying. As the doctors and nurses worked together, God used them to heal, and three members of his family accepted Christ as their Saviour before he left the hospital.

Eight-year-old Felixi lay so still it was difficult to see him breathe. Many of his joints were swollen and caused excruciating pain. After many weeks of intravenous treatment with powerful antibiotics, he gradually began to improve. The doctors often prayed with his Christian parents, sharing that God had a special plan for Felixi, whose life had been spared in such a marvelous way. As Felixi recuperated, the Forts gave him Sunday School literature to read, a songbook, and a Bible. They explained that God had performed a miracle of healing in his life and that he owed his life to God. Wana Ann's heart leaped for joy as she walked down the hospital hall, arm around Felixi's shoulders, on the day he left to return home.

Morning clinic had been busy. Wana Ann and a BSU summer missionary medical student were ready to leave for a late lunch when orderlies wheeled in a 34-year-old man on a stretcher. A swift glance told them their late lunch would be, at best, an early supper!

The critically ill man was semiconscious, his body burning with fever. The muscles in his face and arms twitched uncontrollably. A quick examination revealed a stiff neck and pneumonia. Upon speaking with his brother, Wana Ann discovered that Mairos had been ill for more than three weeks. Several visits to the *nganga*, with his treatments of cuts on the chest to relieve the pain, had not helped. Mairos had become worse; a severe headache led to light seizures, then unconsciousness.

The brother tried to explain the three week delay. Mairos's family believed the *nganga* would help them appease the unhappy *mudzimu* (family spirit) responsible for his illness. Besides, the family lived many miles from any medical doctor or clinic, a long journey to make on a bicycle. Finally, however, a family member did ride to Sanyati to ask for the ambulance.

After Mairos was placed in a hospital bed and given initial medical treatment, Wana Ann spoke with his brother. She explained the seriousness of the illness and told him Mairos's chances for recovery would have been much greater if he had come sooner.

"Are you Christians?" inquired Wana Ann.

"Oh, no," answered Wiri. "We've never been to any church. I don't guess we've ever heard a sermon."

Wana Ann's heart cried out to God to perform a miracle so that the desperately ill man would at least have an opportunity to hear about Jesus. She prayed at Mairos's bedside for his recovery and for him and Wiri to find new life in Christ. Wiri listened quietly but said nothing as Wana Ann left the room.

Days passed and, to Wana Ann's trained eyes, Mairos showed a few signs of improvement: his pulse was slower, his temperature lower, and his twitchings controlled. Wiri, however, could not see much change. Mairos was still semiconscious, fed by a tube, and thrashed around in bed when disturbed.

Wana Ann knew Africans found it hard to understand any illness that lasted longer than a few days. Convinced that the sickness would not respond to the *varungu's muti* (white man's medicine), he concluded the illness was an African disease caused by an unhappy *mudzimu*. Before the sickness could be cured, whatever was angering the mudzimu had to be discovered and then atoned for. She knew Wiri was getting tired of caring for his brother. So, it came as no surprise when Wiri informed her that he had decided to take Mairos home.

Missionary nurse Mary Clark enjoyed watching the drama that unfolded as Wana Ann, through much arm waving and many agitated cries in Shona, convinced Wiri that Mairos could not leave the hospital.

"This disease can affect the *varungu* as well as the *vatema* (white people as well as black). If your *nganga* could not cure him the first three weeks of his illness, he certainly can't help him now. I cannot guarantee that Mairos will recover, but we are claiming God's power to help and he is receiving the proper medicine. He must receive his treatment in this hospital." Needless to say, no one ever suggested again that Mairos should go home.

Three weeks later, Mairos's spinal fluid was clear. After several more weeks, his lung healed completely. What a joy to see Mairos sitting in a wheelchair in the sunshine. Daily Wana Ann thanked God for Mairos's progress and continued to pray for his complete recovery and salvation.

Each day Mairos and Wiri heard the gospel over the hospital's public address system. Both attended chapel when Mairos was well enough. Chaplain Semwayo frequently visited and prayed for Mairos. He explained the way of salvation to Mairos, Wiri, and their uncle who came to visit. Before Mairos went home, all three accepted Christ as their Saviour.

Chaplain Semwayo wrote a letter about the new Christians to the lay leader of the little Baptist church at Nenyuka, a village in Tonga country near the brothers' home. Later he received a reply, thanking him for writing about Wiri and Mairos. They were faithfully attending the services at Nenyuka and were baptized by missionary Bud Fray.

Once again the Forts were reminded of their purpose and that of the Sanyati Baptist Hospital. God gave the privilege to be used to heal the sick, but that was only part of the task. The greatest privilege was being used to present Jesus Christ to lost people who came to the hospital. What a blessing when those who found Jesus returned to their villages, became a part of a church there, and witnessed to their own people!

Information in this chapter was taken from the following articles written by Wana Ann Fort for the *Commission*: "Why Have a Mission Hospital" (December 1958), pp. 10, 32; "That They Might See" (September 1964), pp. 10-11; "Two Months in Rhodesia" (December 1968); pp. 14-17; and "The Brothers" (February 1972), pp. 10-11. Other *Commission* articles used were "Joe's Place" (August 1975), pp. 14-17, written by M. Giles Fort; and "Sanyati: Celebrating 25 Years, Hoping for the Future" (January 1979), pp. 16-17, written by Ruth Fowler.

9

CHURCH BUILDERS

*A*sign stretched across the baptistery proclaiming the theme for the quarterly weekend meeting of the Sanyati Baptist Church: *Ndichavaka Chechi Yangu* (I Will Build My Church). Sitting in the church on a bench crowded with some of the many people who had come for the meeting, four-year-old Gregg Fort wiggled and squirmed restlessly. Beside him sat his mother, holding little brother Grady.

After studying the banner for awhile, Gregg asked in a loud whisper, "Mother, what does that sign say?" Wana Ann quietly explained that the sign told the people that during the meeting they would be studying ways God wanted His church to grow. Since, at age four, growing is of utmost importance, young Gregg was instantly intrigued. After several minutes of deep concentration, he asked with a puzzled look, "But, Mother, how can a church grow?" His literal mind, try as it might, just could not picture the walls and roof of the church building growing at all!

Wana Ann, however, sat thinking. "Here is a church, God's church, that has truly grown." She remembered meeting outside under that big mahogany tree during the first years at Sanyati. During the rainy season, the church crowded into a classroom in the school building, feeling like sardines before the two- or three-hour service ended. Through the years, Wana Ann had become quite good at stuffing each of her young sons with jelly beans to keep them quiet during the long Shona service.

Money from the Lottie Moon Christmas Offering provided the material to build the church building. There were not enough funds remaining to pay a contractor, so Giles and an African builder set to work. The church was built in 1956, using unskilled laborers. God certainly blessed their efforts; the building looked like a professional built it.

God's blessings upon the early work of the church was evident at this quarterly meeting. Members and visitors had come from five different preaching stations to spend two nights sleeping on pallets in the back of the church building.

They would cook their meals outside.

At the 8:30 morning Sunday School, Africans and missionaries worked together to teach the Bible to children and adults in 12 different classes. Even now, growth continued as the worship service concluded. Fourteen new members were received by letter and five persons accepted Christ as their Saviour.

Another bright spot for the Forts had been their work with the Gowe Church. The church had voted to move its meeting place from a tree in Gowe to a tree in Tilcor Township at the big irrigation scheme. A revival was held there for the Tonga and Shona people, resulting in a regular Tonga service, led by Giles, under another tree. Pastor Charlie Chitofu preached the Shona service.

The Gowe residents later decided that walking to Tilcor Township took too long. They began another service at Gowe. The Forts and Pastor Chitofu went to Tilcor first on Sunday morning, then to Gowe, and finally back home around four in the afternoon. The people started a building fund and began making bricks for the new church building.

Several families from Sanyati Baptist Church moved to a new area, 20 miles in the opposite direction of the Mission station. One deacon, Baba Israel Mutengo, started church services in this new area and organized a Sunday School and WMU as well. How exciting to see the New Testament pattern of church growth at work in Sanyati! Maviru Baptist Church met in a village school and the Forts visited there occasionally, helping take literature and encouraging them.

Early one Sunday morning, unaware of the unique worship experience awaiting her, Wana Ann climbed into the pickup truck. She drove seven miles to meet some members of WMU at Gowe Baptist Church. They were concerned about Mai Chifanah because her husband constantly squandered the family funds on beer, providing little for his family. They had decided to take Mai Chifanah gifts of food. Her baby had also been ill.

As Wana Ann parked the truck, one of the Baptist men met her and guided her across the field and playing ground to Mai Chifanah's home. How surprised she was to find a dozen or more men from Gowe Church there with the women. They had decided to come and hold a special service before church time. There in their midst stood Baba Israel, having cycled 22 miles to attend this special service.

As the group sat down on old sacks and mats under a tree and began to sing, a few large raindrops splashed upon their faces. Clouds quickly gathered; the driving rain forced the crowd to gather up their mats and move into the breezeway that separated the two rooms of the Chifanah home.

Wana Ann found herself jammed into a corner, her left side shoved against an open grillwork. She was surrounded on other sides by 14 women and their babies. Little children sat on the floor in one room, while the older boys and overflow of men sat in the other room. One woman thoughtfully placed a big towel over Wana Ann's legs, since her navy blue WMU uniform skirt was caught under some of the women around her. It was the towel she used to secure her baby on her back and was rather damp, but Wana Ann was touched by her assistance.

Everyone's spirits were jubilant; the singing was joyous. As Baba Israel began to speak, Wana Ann's soul rejoiced in the presence of her Lord and her heart worshiped Him. Suddenly, she became aware of her surroundings: seated in a cramped position, covered with a damp towel, a cold wind blowing misty rain onto her left shoulder. To her amazement, she realized how little her surroundings mattered as she worshiped.

At the end of the service, four young men made public decisions to accept Christ. The torrential rain made travel to the usual church meeting place impossible. Instead, the people remained together and continued to sing, pray, and fellowship.

Mai Chifanah brought out two clay pots of *mahewu*, a drink made from cornmeal, flour, sugar, millet, and water. It had a sour taste because it was mixed the day before it was served. Wana Ann was usually able to graciously decline *mahewu* and drink something else, but in this humble home, there was nothing else. She managed to swap the huge, brimming-full cup she received for a small, half-filled cup and was able to drink it all with a smile. She returned home rejoicing. Realizing that many times events occurred that were discouraging— churches sometimes did not grow as strong as they should, people who accepted Christ sometimes backslid, and at times it appeared that the devil was winning a victory— she was thankful for the opportunity to worship the Lord in spirit and in truth with a group of His own children. She knew that God was in control of the work and received glory and victory from the service and worship of His children.

Information in this chapter was taken from "Little Comfort, Deep Worship," *The Commission* (January 1976), p. 27, written by Wana Ann Fort.

Giles poses proudly with the five boys.

10

ANOTHER LOTTIE MOON

*T*he pecan pie baking in the oven filled the African air with a luscious aroma. As Wana Ann turned the pages in her recipe book to replace the old blue air letter on which the recipe was written, she envisioned the sparkling blue eyes and heard those oft-repeated words, "I take second place to no one with my pecan pie!", as she remembered the dear cook who shared her recipe.

Wana Ann first met Mrs. H. E. Long, Sr., who later became her adopted "Auntie Lou," when she spoke for an associational WMU meeting in Shreveport, Louisiana, in 1957. It was the Forts' first furlough and Wana Ann considered herself green and inexperienced as a missionary speaker. Mrs. Long's warmth and enthusiasm immediately made Wana Ann feel relaxed and accepted. It quickly became obvious that Mrs. Long had a deep love for missions, missionaries, and WMU. It was easy to love Auntie Lou.

During the Forts' second furlough, they lived in Shreveport, Louisiana, to enable Giles to take a year's residency in ophthalmology. Wana Ann began receiving Auntie Lou Long's delicious "world's best" pecan pies and learning what her love for missions meant. It meant doing and giving, especially giving to the Lottie Moon Christmas Offering.

In the fall of that year, Auntie Lou was already planning how to get all the men in her church who could afford it to give $100 each to the Lottie Moon Christmas Offering. She also had this amount as her own personal offering goal. She had been a widow for several years and inflation affected the value of her pension money. Sometimes it was hard for her to meet her goal, but she smiled glowingly today as she displayed a newspaper clipping for Wana Ann.

A men's service club in Shreveport had made Auntie Lou the recipient of their annual award: a lovely gold watch. Her eyes twinkled as she said, "That watch was too small for an old woman like me to tell the time anyway, so I just sold it for Lottie Moon."

She was always happy to lend Wana Ann her

old treadle sewing machine. "I don't sew much anymore. Next year I'm going to sell the machine for Lottie Moon."

When she arranged for Wana Ann to speak for a week of prayer luncheon, she seemed to be doing a dozen jobs at once. Discussing her enthusiasm and concern for missions, one of the women said, "You know, you just might as well call her Miss Lottie Moon."

Several times that furlough Wana Ann and Auntie Lou visited. Her sons and their families were very dear to her, but she maintained a fierce independence. She held a deep love for them all and delighted in showing her family pictures. She felt at ease discussing her handicapped grandson, since she knew that Grady, the Forts' youngest son, had Down's syndrome. Together, they shared their experiences with the Lord in those times of heartache. They also shared another common bond: neither had a daughter.

When Wana Ann returned to Sanyati, she sent Auntie Lou carbon copies of the Forts' weekly family letters. Auntie Lou loved them and sent chatty letters in return.

The Forts' next furlough in 1965 was just in time for the Week of Prayer for Foreign Missions. Auntie Lou had been pestering her pastor to get the Forts signed up early to speak to their church. She met Wana Ann with the words, "I keep telling the Lord I'm getting old and have just a few more years. I tell Him to be sure to let me die at Lottie Moon Christmas Offering time since I plan to be buried with an offering envelope in each hand. When all those people march by my coffin I'll be telling them to produce those $100 bills. None of that wasted money on flowers for me." Wana Ann assured her she would do more good sticking around to tell all those people in person.

The Forts had a custom of giving any honorarium or love offering they received during Christmas to the churches where they spoke, asking that the money be added to the church's missions offering. They felt that this was a way they could share in God's world missions program and it provided a deep inner joy for them. However, most of the time, the church people would refuse their gifts, saying they should use the money for themselves. Not Auntie Lou.

She gave Wana Ann the check; Wana Ann signed it over to the church and returned it to a beaming Auntie Lou. "Well, I tried to get the committee to give you more money than this, but they felt we needed to keep some for other expenses," explained Auntie Lou. "If they had just listened to me, we'd have even more for the Lottie Moon Christmas Offering."

That Christmas, Wana Ann discussed what she could give Auntie Lou with a friend who said, "She is really having a hard time getting the money together for her own offering this year. One year she sold her old car and gave that money, but I don't know what she plans now. I think she would rather have money than anything else." Wana Ann took over a card containing $25 well before Christmas. Auntie Lou grinned when she opened it but gave no clue as to how she would spend it.

Two months later an excited Auntie Lou told Wana Ann what had happened. She had put away the gift in a safe place until she could take it to church. When she went to retrieve it, it was not where she remembered. She searched frantically, then concluded it had been stolen. She quietly replaced it with her own dwindling funds.

"And guess what?" she demanded. "Just yesterday I was cleaning the closet and there in an old white purse I found the envelope and the money. I guess I'll just keep it for next year's offering."

Soon afterward, Auntie Lou fell and broke her arm. During her visit at the hospital, Wana Ann brushed and braided Auntie Lou's hair. Auntie Lou couldn't stop grinning. "Just think. The great Dr. Wana Ann Fort is my hairdresser. I just wish everyone could see me now."

"Funny thing," thought Wana Ann. "To dear Auntie Lou, I am a great person. Not because of who I am or anything I have done, but because God has chosen me to be His missionary. Auntie Lou feels that way about every missionary, that they are all the greatest."

As Wana Ann remembered Auntie Lou's faithfulness, she felt a deep sense of loss as she realized Auntie Lou was no longer praying daily for them. She often faced a difficult situation strengthened by the knowledge that Auntie Lou was praying for her. She was certain no missionary had a more faithful intercessor than Auntie Lou had been during her life.

Now Auntie Lou had gone on to heaven. Her son wrote the Forts a touching letter at her death.

"I grew up in WMU. My first recollection was at the age of three. I remember lots of women present, lots of talking, which I endured, and then strawberry shortcake with whipped cream after the meeting. I remember something was said at Christmastime about a 'Miss Moon' and they passed the offering plate. It meant nothing to me. Later as an Royal Ambassador I memorized Scriptures and learned about David Livingstone and other missionaries. Each December there was a Lottie Moon Christmas Offering. It still meant nothing to me.

"Shortly after I came back from service at the age of 23, my father died. That left Mother lonely but with lots of time . . . time to put a map of the world on our dining room wall and pinpoint missionaries in different parts of the world. She prayed for them daily, wrote them often, and sent hard-to-get goodies to them at Christmas. She always, always plugged Lottie Moon. It became embarrassing. She was such a fanatic but missionaries didn't mean a thing to me.

"A few years later she asked me to take her to Glorieta in New Mexico for Foreign Missions Week. I knew how much she would enjoy it but also how dull and boring it would be for me. We went. After that week, missionaries and Lottie

Moon took on a real meaning for me. I met several real, live missionaries, heard their experiences and saw the caliber of people they were.

"I finally understood about missionaries . . . and Lottie Moon. I knew then the importance of Lottie Moon Christmas Offering, and my mother's zeal for this offering. She always had a big supply of Lottie Moon envelopes. She knew who could give $100 and would approach these men at the church and tell them, 'If you'll give $100 to Lottie Moon, I'll bake you a pecan pie.' You can't imagine how many pies she baked! This was until she was 80 years of age when she fell and began going down. But she could still pray for missionaries and talk up Lottie Moon.

"Mother fell again and had several light strokes. She had been in a nursing home several years. When I saw her recently she was just about gone . . . just about everything had played out except her strong heart. No expression on her face . . . just a blank . . . but when I told her I had recently attended a National Prayer Breakfast where there were 1,500 men present to pray for the missionaries and Lottie Moon, she smiled for just a moment.

"Last night just as the new year was beginning, Mother slipped away to eternal happiness and I'm sure to a great reunion with old missionary friends and loved ones. If anyone would like to do something in memory of Mrs. H. E. Long, give to the Lottie Moon Christmas Offering for Foreign Missions through your church. It's not too late, and

. . . who knows . . . when you get to heaven, a pecan pie may be awaiting you there."[1]

Auntie Lou didn't get her wish to die at Lottie Moon Christmas Offering time, but Wana Ann and Giles sent a gift to her church in her memory that went for the Lottie Moon Christmas Offering. Wana Ann could almost hear her scolding from heaven itself if they had thought of doing anything else!

[1]Wallace Long, "I Finally Understood About Missionaries," *Baptist Message,* 17 January 1974, p. 7.

Wana Ann and a bashful GA at the Baptist camp at Gwelo during a GA convention.

11

THE FOUR-OF-A-KIND CLUB

*M*ilton Giles Fort, III, was born in April 1952, six years after his parents were married. In October of that year, his parents were appointed as missionaries to Southern Rhodesia in Africa. His new home would be in the Sanyati Reserve, primitive bush country located 70 miles from the nearest town. His parents would build a Baptist hospital in this remote area.

The precious raven-haired baby prompted many prayers of protection to be offered in his behalf: protection from malaria and other tropical diseases, and protection from cobras, mambas, and adders. Pleas of "Surely you're not going to take that precious child with you to that wild country!'' prompted smiles from Wana Ann and Giles, despite the apprehension in their hearts. They replied, "God gave him to us and we must trust God to care for him now."

A cold winter day found little Gilesie leaving on a ship bound for Sanyati. What fun! The ship's officers gave him a full tour, which included an opportunity to turn all the knobs on the radio switchboard. Upon reaching Sanyati, Gilesie had a great time living with Aunt Betty and Uncle Ralph Bowlin (MKs always called other missionaries "Aunt" and "Uncle"). Daniel, the cook, and Margaret, the young girl who watched Gilesie outside to keep the snakes away, became fine friends and playmates for him.

Soon brother David joined the Fort family in 1954. Brother Gordon arrived in 1955 and little brother Gregg was born in 1959. Gilesie decided boys were best, since girls didn't always play with boys and he was blessed with a ready-made play group. The four Fort boys soon became a part of the Four-of-a-Kind Club. Two other missionary families in Southern Rhodesia each had four children of the same sex; the Robert E. Beaty boys, the Gerald S. Harvey girls, and the Fort boys comprised a unique group of missionary children. Later the Harveys had a fifth daughter and the Forts a fifth son!

The brothers enjoyed playing in the huge sand-piles in the back yard, watching the fish swim and frolic in the goldfish pond, accompanying their father as he supervised the building of Sanyati Baptist Hospital, riding their bicycles, and adventuring with Daddy on exciting hunting trips. Sunday School and Sunbeam Band with African friends were eagerly anticipated each week. And of course there was always someone around to join in a game of Kick the Can, Cowboys and Indians, or Capture the Flag.

The boys always looked forward to evening meals. Dinner was served by candlelight on china plates and a linen tablecloth. Fresh cut flowers always graced the table and classical music played softly in the background. This was Daddy's family time—a time to withdraw from the hospital, its pressures and demands; a time to be together as a family, sharing the important events and concerns of the day. Everyone remained at the table until the last candle was snuffed out, reluctant to face studies, chores, or bedtime.

Young Giles began correspondence school in 1958. He and another MK, Mary Esther Small, were the only pupils. It was fun to learn in a tiny classroom made from a building intended for a chicken house. It was great to have Mother for a teacher!

When David began correspondence school, the classes grew from two to four. The Smalls had transferred to Zambia, and the Marion Fray family arrived with their children, Carol and Jerry. One school day Wana Ann asked David and Jerry where they would like to be if they could choose anywhere in the world. Both answered without hesitating, "We'd rather be right here where we are. We like Sanyati. We can ride our bicycles everywhere without worrying about cars or people. We can climb trees. We have things to do and places to play. It's fun to feed the monkeys that come to play in our yard."

The brothers enthusiastically awaited Mission meeting time each year. They delighted in playing with all the other missionary children and joining them for Vacation Bible School. The children were taught by missionaries and missionary journeymen while their parents planned the work for the Southern Rhodesia Baptist Mission for the coming year. At the end of VBS, the children shared what they had learned with their parents. One particular year held sweet memories.

The Junior-Intermediate part of the VBS program was introduced by David Fort. "Moms and Dads, this is for you. We have the title "MK" because of you and we're proud of it. We wish to present in song some of our thoughts and feelings about the missions field."

As Carol Fray and Wesley Neely provided a ukulele accompaniment, the children sang "The MK Song," written for them by journeyman Connie Roediger.

Our parents heard the call of God and followed
    His command
To preach the Gospel, sweet and pure through-
    out a distant land.
Of course, we too have followed; and in this
    place called home,

We too are sharing in the task: to make Christ
  Jesus known!
For we are MKs. We're proud to tell it. . . .
We'll live for Him, Christ Jesus, Our Lord.
It was a VBS commencement night misty-eyed
parents would not forget.

Wana Ann stood by the bed of a sick child
during a famine and tried to assure the mother of
God's love. She thought, "This mother wonders
how I can possibly understand. I have never seen
one of my sons dying from malnutrition. What
do I know of suffering?"

Then, the fifth Fort son, Grady, was born.
Wana Ann was immediately aware that there was
a problem. Her doctor mind said "mongoloid,"
while her mother's heart refused to consider it.

Three days after his birth, Giles came into the
nursery and sat in the rocker as Wana Ann stood
quietly by Grady's crib. "We've got to talk to the
Lord about this," he pleaded with Wana Ann. As
they bowed their heads, Giles asked God to make
them teachable in this difficult situation.

Later that day, two African women arrived saying, "We know your baby is not all right."

"No," admitted Wana Ann, "he is not all
right."

"It is our custom when people are sick or in
sorrow to come and pray with them," they said.
"We have come to pray with you."

The sweet, comforting presence of the Holy
Spirit filled Wana Ann's room that afternoon. In

her heart she knew that, even though her son was not all right, God was going to make her experience with little Grady all right. Grady opened more doors for Wana Ann and Giles to witness than any other experience in their lives.

As Grady made his place in the family, his big brothers taught him what being a boy was all about. Big brother Giles enjoyed stamp collecting and hunting with his friends. David delighted in taking care of the Fort family zoo. There was Babe Ruth, the gigantic chameleon, and Walter and Squeaky Tweety, the baby rats that were fed with a medicine dropper. Gordon and Gregg were always adding to the collection with assorted frogs, chameleons, and millipedes. Gregg amused himself with his African friends, catching birds, trapping field mice, and eating *sadza* and *muriwo*. He also enjoyed the African delicacy of roasted termites, much to the dismay of his mother! All five boys shared at least one common interest—Mother's yummy hand-cranked, homemade ice cream.

Finally the day arrived to load the "Green Hornet" (the Dodge town wagon) and drive the 250 miles to Bulawayo to take Giles and David to boarding school. Eleven-year-old Giles and nine-year-old David were thrilled to buy the official school uniform: khaki shorts, short-sleeved shirts, school cap, tie, belt, sweater, stockings, blazer, brown shoes, and even white cricket boots. Wana Ann lovingly labeled, folded and packed each garment.

Upon arriving at the school, Wana Ann and the boys greeted the headmaster and several teachers, paid the necessary fees, and then ventured to the younger boys' dormitory. They climbed the stairs and spoke to the matron, who agreed to allow the boys to stay together. Later Giles would move into the middle boys' dorm.

A pair of misty brown eyes and a pair of misty blue ones met Wana Ann's. Quick hugs followed. Wana Ann exited swiftly down the stairs, suppressing the urge to gather her eldest sons into her arms and take them back to Sanyati. She realized the day would quickly come when the other three would also say good-bye. It was not a pleasant thought. Each good-bye would prove more difficult, with each leaving the house a bit quieter, a great deal emptier, and far too neat and tidy. School holidays, however, would soon return things at home to their lively state. They had two four-week holidays and six weeks home in December and January.

The family motto, Good, Better, Best . . . Never Let it Rest . . . Until Your Good is Better . . . and Your Better is the Best!, had a serious impact upon the Fort boys. Giles participated in sports and studied hard, with subjects ranging from English, math, science, French, Latin, history, and geography to art and woodwork. All that hard work naturally led to "end of term fun," a time to engage in mischievous pranks to relieve tension. At graduation, he received the Milton Award for overall contribution to his school in leadership, activities, and sports. He was head of Pioneer House, his boarding dorm.

David's years of diligent study were rewarded when he received the Milton Honours. The award was rarely given by his school and recognized excellence in moral standards, character, leadership, scholastic achievement, and athletic performance. He was head boy of Hillride Primary School and Deputy Head of Milton High School.

Gordon accepted God's call to be a minister during his years at boarding school and was an active witness among his many school friends. He served at his primary school as class president, or head boy. He, too, excelled in athletics—rugby, judo, and basketball, and was at the top of his class academically.

Gregg attended high school in Gwelo, 150 miles from Sanyati, and lived at an MK home. Fourteen MKs lived at the home, along with the houseparents. The house was in walking distance to the school. It was exciting to live with other MKs, many of whom had lived in Sanyati. Each day included time for study and chores. The girls helped with cooking and cleaning; the boys helped with shoe shining, gardening, and odd jobs. There was still plenty of time for rugby, cricket, hockey, basketball, and tennis. Gregg especially enjoyed rugby, tennis, and chess. Because of the political situation in Rhodesia, Gregg transferred to Treverton in South Africa for his last 1½ years. His senior year he was co-head boy of his dorm. And, then, of course, he was school dux, or valedictorian.

Grady's first love was music. He attended the Hopelands School in Bulawayo and participated in the plays, pantomimes, and light musical performances staged by the school. He was always happy, optimistic, and loving.

Yet another kind of good-bye came in 1971. The Fort family waited in the air terminal, chatting about insignificant things to pass the time. Wana Ann glanced lovingly at her firstborn, unable to think of much to say. She teasingly asked if he had any last-minute advice or requests.

Dark eyes twinkling, he responded, "I guess not, unless you might send me some addressed envelopes." He had just received a handful with explicit instructions on writing home!

The flight was called and good-byes exchanged. David called, "Cheers, Giles!" as Wana Ann and Giles walked with him to the exit, hugged him and watched him walk away . . . alone. Wana Ann stood, her heart overflowing with love and sadness. Broad shoulders, strong and trim from rugby, dark hair tumbling into a mass of curls— a precious young man on his way to a new life at Texas A & M University in the States.

It seemed impossible that 18 years had passed since a young Gilesie first set foot on African soil. It helped to have young Grady, whose ears hurt from the noise of the jet engines, to console. The engines roared and the plane slowly rolled away. It gained speed, then lifted swiftly into the black night sky.

As the Forts turned and started back to the car, they laughingly played their game of "counting the boys" to be sure one wasn't left behind. Now there were only four. As Wana Ann struggled with her loneliness, she realized again how God did not call His children to an easy way, but promised something infinitely more precious. How she praised and trusted Him for His grace sufficient to meet her every need.

Information from this chapter was taken from the March 1961 *Commission* article, "I'm Glad I'm a Medical M.K." pp. 16-18; written by Wana Ann Fort for her son, M. Giles Fort III.

12

ARCHIE'S DREAM LIVES ON

We had some difficult times," Wana Ann said, reflecting on saying good-bye to her firstborn.

"But God was always with us," Giles said thoughtfully.

"Yes," Wana Ann responded. "Even when Archie was killed."

They fell silent then, remembering their martyred friend and the war that separated them from Sanyati.

Reports that the *vakomana* were coming across the Zambian border reached the Sanyati Mission station just as the Forts prepared to go on furlough. *Vakomana*, or "boys" in the Shona language, was the name given to the Rhodesian freedom fighter guerrillas, most of whom were teenagers. In recent years, guerrilla activity had increased as the freedom fighters and the white minority government forces battled for control of Rhodesia's government.

Wana Ann and Giles left for America on May 9, 1978, feeling the Sanyati compound was safe. It was located in the center of Rhodesia and most of the guerrilla activity had been near Mozambique in the east. Clinics in the outlying missions areas had been curtailed earlier because of their remoteness, however, and in the first few years there had been guerrilla incursions throughout the area.

At the meeting of the Baptist Mission of Rhodesia in early May, many missionaries shared their testimonies of how they felt they were in God's perfect will as they performed the tasks He had called them to do. They felt an umbrella of God's protection over the work in Sanyati and Gokwe. In the history of Southern Baptist missions work there had been only a few violent deaths of missionaries, in spite of their service in several war-torn areas. So, it was only natural that Giles left his work clothes in the closet so he could get back to work immediately when he returned from furlough.

Shock and dismay filled their hearts, however, when they received word a month later that their friend and co-worker, Archie Dunaway, had been murdered. He had been killed on June 16 on the grounds of the Sanyati Baptist compound. It was especially distressing because the Dunaways were among the strongest of the missionaries at Sanyati in their belief that God's hand was upon their work.

The Dunaways had served in Africa for 31 years, going first to Nigeria for 20 years and then to Rhodesia in 1971. Archie served as maintenance supervisor and area evangelist at the Sanyati Mission station. Margaret was both nurse and director of the school for midwives. The Forts considered them to be good pioneer-type missionaries. Margaret was a competent nurse and Archie fixed and built things as well as he did evangelism.

The Forts received more details surrounding the tragedy. Margaret had been hard at work, preparing the first graduating class of the midwifery school for oral examinations. She left home early in the chilly morning, knowing Archie would meet her in the car at the hospital at six that evening. When Archie failed to meet her at their customary time and place, she immediately sensed something was wrong.

After a thorough but fruitless search by the missionaries, security forces were notified. Margaret called her son John in Nashville, Tennessee, to alert him to the situation and ask him and his church to pray.

Archie's body was found the next morning, 13 hours after he was discovered missing. He had been brutally beaten and bayoneted to death by guerrillas.

Immediate action began at the Sanyati Mission station. All missionary personnel were asked to evacuate the Sanyati compound. Giles was saddened to realize how badly the medical missions program would be disrupted by the war.

He was concerned that the 300,000 tribe members living in the Sanyati reserve would be without medical care if the hospital could not continue. When the Forts left for furlough, only a very few medical missionaries of all denominations were still in Southern Rhodesia, a dramatic decrease from the approximately 80 present just six years before.

When the white minority government declared independence from Britain in 1965, and as border skirmishes with nationalist guerrillas expanded into war, Baptist missionaries had to guard against taking any type of political action. The missionaries considered themselves guests of the government and avoided taking any political stand.

Church services consisted solely of preaching and teaching the Bible. The Forts were aware of government-sent people who attended services in Sanyati just to hear what was being said. Because political questions were not addressed from the pulpit, the Sanyati Mission maintained good relations with the government and the nationalists.

The recent increase in guerrilla activity was due to the upcoming election in Rhodesia, where the government would likely be replaced by black majority rule.

As the Forts considered their 25 years of service in Sanyati, they were comforted to know that, at least for the present, trained African residents were conducting the work of the hospital, schools, and churches. The 100-bed hospital had African medical assistants, pharmacy and service personnel, as well as a Rhodesian director of nursing. All of the churches in the Sanyati area had local pastors. John Monroe and Maurice Randall were flying out to Sanyati two days a week to take care of dental and surgical needs. They commuted by plane, Randall from Gatooma 60 miles east of Sanyati, and Monroe from Gwelo, 150 miles away.

The decision to evacuate the Sanyati Mission had had no effect on the Baptist Mission's urban work in Salisbury, Bulawayo, Gwelo, Fort Victoria, Triangle, and Gatooma.

However, later guerilla activity forced the evacuation of the Baptist Seminary located 12 miles from Gwelo. A number of missionary families transferred to other countries. Traveling to churches even in the cities was severely curtailed. The Forts realized the danger and persecution faced by their Christian African friends. They knelt together to pray for Rhodesia, needing themselves the assurance of victory in Jesus. As they prayed for a peaceful transition and continued freedom to preach the gospel, they claimed the truth that only Jesus could break down the barriers that separated people.

As they joined hands, grieved by the loss of their friend, their hearts longed to return to Rhodesia and the people they loved. With the uncertainty of the future hanging over them, they celebrated what God had done in 25 years and what they believed He would continue to do. At the end of their furlough, they hoped to return to the work where God had placed and used them, to see Sanyati Baptist Hospital and the Gokwe Baptist clinics ministering to people in Jesus' name. They hoped to spend the remainder of their missionary career as a part of the ministry at Sanyati.

Until that time, Giles would continue his training in anesthesiology at Parkland Hospital in Dallas, Texas, preparing himself for yet another avenue of medical ministry. The sick and those lost without Christ would still be waiting in Sanyati. The last 25 years would not be erased, even if Sanyati Baptist Hospital closed. The churches and the changed lives would remain as an eternal testament to the love and power of God at work in the lives of the people who gave their life in ministry there, and of the work done at Sanyati Baptist Mission. The Forts' dream and Archie's dream would still live on!

13

BUILDING NEW DREAMS

*W*hy go back? Isn't nearly 30 years of service enough?

These questions were voiced many times as the Forts prepared to return to Rhodesia, now called Zimbabwe. Recent changes had occurred since a new government had been elected. Pastors who had fled from persecution were returning. Church groups were meeting openly again, many under trees near their demolished church buildings. Refugees from the war were returning to take up their broken lives with nothing more than the tattered clothing they wore.

God's call was crystal clear to Wana Ann and

Giles, leading them back to minister to people who had suffered greatly during the war. Missionary personnel had dropped over 50 percent. Many rural church buildings, clinics, schools, and businesses were destroyed by the guerrillas. Numerous people were without Bibles and hymnals, which had been destroyed by guerrillas or by termites as they lay buried in the fields.

The Forts deplored the reports of the murders of many African friends. Baba Cain, father of six and a faithful worker at Sanyati Mission station, was stopped on his way home. His arms were cut off and thrown, along with his mutilated body, into a crocodile-infested river.

Kuda KwaShe, a young lay preacher, was taken from his hut and young bride in the middle of the night. Called a "sellout" for preaching Jesus, he was killed with a pickax as he knelt to pray. Many others followed the early disciples' examples of being faithful unto death. Wana Ann and Giles yearned to return to be a part of God's continuing ministry in Zimbabwe, to help ease some of the hurts and problems.

As they returned, although circumstances and conditions were different, their commission, their message, and their God remained the same. Arriving on September 27, 1980, they began to work with the churches in the Salisbury area, as well as with the Zimbabwe government hospital located there.

New experiences greeted the Forts upon their arrival in Salisbury. Giles was able to put his newly acquired training to use immediately as he began work as honorary senior registrar in anesthesiology at the medical college and government hospitals. The chore of moving into a new home awaited Wana Ann.

The Mission house was located in Waterfalls, a suburb of Salisbury. The Forts' possessions had been moved from Sanyati to storage in Salisbury during the month following Archie Dunaway's murder. Missing bedroom furniture, a mattress, office furniture, and dining room chairs made shopping for replacements a necessity. Missing bicycles, garden tools, buckets, pots, and pans were an inconvenience to rectify.

Although everything was not there, the Forts were grateful for what they did find. Once again they were reminded of the relative unimportance of things. Thankful for what God provided to make life comfortable, they rejoiced in the awareness that their joy in Christ was not dependent upon material things.

The large, spacious yard of their new home was filled with beautiful flowers and was a delight to behold. The generous supply of large windows gave Wana Ann the immediate task of making curtains. Of course, there was the seemingly endless task of sorting through and finding spots for box after box of accumulated household items.

The words found in Nehemiah 2:20 kept racing through Giles' head as he flew with Missionary Aviation Fellowship pilot Gordon Marshall over the Gokwe area: "The God of heaven, he will prosper us; therefore we his servants will arise and build." (KJV). One after another, they flew over clinic and church sites, familiar places Giles had visited many times. Places where, during clinic times, the Word was preached and people accepted Christ as Saviour; places where Sunday worship services were held; where mothers were taught to care for their children; where obstetrical patients were examined and high-risk pregnancies detected, so the mothers could deliver their babies safely at Sanyati Baptist Hospital.

It devastated Giles to see all but two clinics completely destroyed, lying in ruins. Clinic equipment and furnishings were gone. Church buildings were vandalized and in ruins. It had taken many people more than 15 years to develop and build this work; in two years time, it was all gone.

As the Forts visited with friends, they witnessed the hurt as difficult experiences were recounted. Yet there was rejoicing for the testimony heard time after time: "God delivered us."

Wana Ann was encouraged by the WMU convention at the Baptist encampment at Gwelo. Because of the war, the women had not met together at the camp for two years. How excited they were to be back together again! The program theme was In Everything Give Thanks. Joyful praises filled the air for the freedom to worship and fellowship there. Over 300 Baptist women attended and experienced a deep spirit of renewal and dedication.

During one business session, a vote was taken on the work to be aided by their 1981 gifts for the week of prayer for Zimbabwe. Mrs. Muchechetere, a pastor's wife from Sanyati, spoke of the needs of the Tonga people. Drought had caused much hardship; crops and livestock had been destroyed by the *vakomana*. Moved with compassion by the urgent need, Mrs. Nziramasanga, a pastor's wife from Harare, encouraged the women not to wait until the next year. She exhorted them to go home and collect clothing and money to send to these needy brothers immediately.

Spontaneously, one woman walked forward to lay an offering on the table. Other women joined her, singing the chorus *Batsirai Mumwe* (Help Someone) as they came forward. From their hearts and meager funds came an offering of $72.

Richard Musiyiwa became a Christian as an orphan boy. Obeying God's call to preach, he applied to the Baptist seminary. During school holidays, he earned money to help pay his fees by working at the Sanyati Baptist Hospital as assistant to Chaplain Semwayo. After graduation, he served as chaplain for the Gokwe clinics.

During the war, he and his wife and two little girls fled from their home without any of their possessions. They lived in the Kasirisiri area for a time, then were forced to flee again. In 1980, he was called to pastor the church at Mufakose.

Pastor Musiyiwa brought surprising news when he came to discuss the need for a preacher at

Mufakose Baptist Church during the September 1981 Crusade for Zimbabwe. "I feel led to invite your son Gregg to preach for us in Shona," he announced.

"Mufundisi (Pastor) Musiyiwa, you and the church must pray about God's leading," blurted out Wana Ann. She knew that would be Gregg's last semester at Texas A & M. It would not be easy for him to be away 2½ weeks. Finding money to finance the trip would be even more difficult. Besides, older and more experienced pastors were usually invited to participate in crusades.

"We have already prayed, Mai Fort," replied Mufundisi Musiyiwa. "But we will pray again before we put Gregg Fort's name on the request form from the Evangelism Board."

Wana Ann later marveled at their faith when Mufundisi assured her that Gregg was coming because he and the church knew that it was God's will.

Upon receiving 1 of 22 letters inviting preachers to participate in the crusade, and upon learning how his name was chosen, Gregg Fort and his wife, Donna, knew they must earnestly pray to know God's will. Knowing they could not accomplish all that the invitation required, they agreed that God could! Schedules were rearranged and finances were provided. Mufundisi Musiyiwa and his church were not at all surprised.

How wonderful the time was with Donna and Gregg! Everyone marveled at his freedom in preaching in Shona. After all, it had been four years since he had spoken or heard the Shona language. The many who heard him preach were amazed that a *murungu* (white person) could speak just like a *mutema* (black person). Many people made decisions during that exciting week.

After the first week at Mufakose, Gregg went home to Sanyati to preach at Kasirisiri. During the war, the guerrillas destroyed the stores, community buildings, the school, and the Baptist church. Ten church members had been killed. How the Forts' hearts ached when they arrived for the church service and found nothing left of the large, beautiful church building except bits of the foundation.

Gregg preached for the school during a special assembly. Since the buildings lay in shambles, they stood under the trees for the service. Many children made decisions to follow Christ that morning.

After the crusade, the Forts took a week of vacation to tour some of Zimbabwe with Donna and Gregg. They attended the last day of the annual WMU convention at the Gwelo camp. The women were excited to meet the Forts' *muroora* (daughter-in-law). They jumped, clapped, and sang some of their traditional welcome-to-the-bride songs. In the African culture, the bride joins the family of her husband and this is considered a special blessing. The Forts readily agreed that they had been blessed with three lovely *varoora*, (daughters-in-law) and were praying for Gordon to find the fourth!

Upon learning that Gregg and Donna felt God leading them to serve as missionaries in Zimbabwe, the women again rejoiced and praised God, saying "He is a child of the people and belongs here in Zimbabwe."

As Wana Ann and Giles pondered three decades of service as medical missionaries, they meditated upon their present service. For years, God kept them at Sanyati, a place they loved, working with people they loved. Now God had moved them to a different type of ministry in the large, modern capital city of Harare. Though different, it was still a ministry of extending God's love and care to people who needed Him.

Frequently they met someone they had known at Sanyati. As Wana Ann taught a methods class at the annual associational WMU leadership training course, a woman and her teenaged daughter approached her. The young woman shared how she almost died as a baby, but was treated and saved at Sanyati Baptist Hospital. Her mother had become a Christian through the love and witness she received while at the hospital. The daughter was also a Christian and shared that many members of their family had accepted Jesus.

Giles was content with his work as a doctor in the anesthesia department of the medical college. He worked as honorary senior lecturer and lectured to young doctors in training as well as serving as anesthesiologist in the operating rooms.

Wana Ann attended pediatric rounds and lectures and conducted a clinic at the Simbaredenga

School near Waterfalls for a year. She also served as assistant secretary of the executive committee of the Baptist Convention, writing minutes of the committee and handling correspondence to the churches. Giles served on the convention Brotherhood committee and as the Mission building administrator and member of the finance division.

Both knew the importance of their work with their local church. With the government committed to leadership based on Leninist Marxism, they knew they must teach the children each Sunday how to know Jesus as Saviour and Lord. Many of the 74 three-to-twelve-year-olds in Wana Ann's Sunday School class had indicated their desire to be Christians. She knew they must be taught and nurtured carefully so that they would develop into strong Christian leaders for Zimbabwe. Through them, perhaps, their parents would come to know Christ as Saviour.

Returning to the bright sunshine of Harare after furlough in 1984, the Forts realized a blend of pain and joy. They were members of two very different worlds—the United States and Zimbabwe—both wonderful, both important, both filled with precious family and friends. Both, however, were separated by many miles.

Once while traveling to a WMU executive committee meeting with some of the African women, Wana Ann was asked if the Forts would ever permanently go back to the States. They said, "You are now *pavanhu* (of the people) and should stay here." How difficult it was to leave either of their worlds!

They deeply felt the only real sacrifice offered the Lord in obedience to His call—loneliness, first for parents, family members, and friends; now for four sons, their wives, and their adorable children. How the Forts missed those priceless grandchildren: Rachel Ann, Daniel, and Katie Ann. Knowing without a doubt that Zimbabwe was where God wanted them, however, enabled them to be happy and content in His work.

Their first Sunday back from furlough was spent in worship with Harare Baptist Church. A young man came forward and testified in Shona, "All of you know how hard my heart has been. You know the kind of life I lived. I have been coming to Sunday School and church, but when I heard the Word of God, I let weeds grow in my heart and choke out the Word. Many stones in my heart have kept the seed from growing. Today, with God's help, I am accepting Jesus and pulling up all the weeds. I am carrying away all the stones from my heart. I want the Word of God to grow now." The Forts' homesickness melted away: their faith renewed. It was for this very purpose they had returned.

As the government followed its development of scientific socialism, problems cropped up for the ministry in Zimbabwe. Most frustrating was the difficulty encountered in obtaining renewals of work permits for missionaries already in the country and in securing residence and work permits for newly appointed personnel. There were many delays and few permits approved.

Due to escalating costs of operation, the Foreign Mission Board turned operation of Sanyati Baptist Hospital over to the Baptist Convention of Zimbabwe. The Convention arranged to receive grants-in-aid from the government. However with the financial difficulties experienced by the government, the grants-in-aid were insufficient to meet all the needs of the hospital. The possibility of its closing hung heavily over the missionaries and staff dedicated to its ministry. The hospital was built to meet the needs of the people who were dying without medical care. So many more people lived in the area now. The need for the hospital had increased and the Forts prayed for a miracle to keep the hospital open.

God answered their prayers. The necessary funds were provided. Faithful, capable, talented medical personnel continue to minister and witness of the love of Jesus there.

The year 1985 found Giles and Wana Ann involved in office and administrative responsibilities. Wana Ann served as treasurer of the Zimbabwe Baptist Mission and enjoyed serving as national WMU cosecretary. She also served as secretary for and as a member of the executive committee of Zimbabwe International Network for Nutrition, an organization involved with helping improve the nutritional standards for infants and young children. Her typewriter was heard many evenings, keys busily working late into the night.

Giles served as Mission administrator and worked with the convention Sunday School emphasis for 1986. He led Calvary Baptist Church in Harare to double its number of Sunday School classes, number of teachers, and its Sunday School enrollment. They also were involved with Immanuel Baptist Church, which had been recently organized.

A severe flulike illness proved to be a harbinger of change that would come for the Forts in 1986. After the illness in 1985, Giles gradually developed neck and shoulder pain. This became so severe he was almost incapacitated and unable to work. Locking up their home, they flew to Dallas, Texas, where Giles entered Baylor Hospital for tests in April 1986. Test results revealed cervical discs that had degenerated at two places in his lower neck. Surgery was successfully performed to relieve the pressure on the nerve roots in his neck, thus relieving the excruciating pain. However, he was also diagnosed as having dystonia, a disorder similar to Parkinson's disease, and had to remain for treatment in Dallas.

As Wana Ann awaited the results of his treatment and word on whether they would be able to return to Zimbabwe, they prayed for God's will to be done. Upon learning that they would need to remain in the States and could not return to their beloved country, they continued to lean on the lesson learned long ago: the most important decision in one's life is to accept Jesus Christ as Saviour and Lord and to be obedient to His will.

14

THE DREAM CONTINUES

*U*npacking the crates from Africa had aroused strong memories, feelings, and emotions as Wana Ann and Giles relived their dreams, observing how God had used them and built upon them to reach lost Africans in Zimbabwe. Their hearts overflowed with glorious praises for the experiences where God's power was seen at work, sometimes in very dramatic ways, but often in daily quiet evidences of the presence of His Spirit.

How thankful they were that they were able to continue in His ministry there for 35 years before their retirement, strengthened and equipped by

Him to be what He wanted them to be as He accomplished His will in their lives.

Their dreams continued through the ministry of their sons. They shared once again the letter Gordon had written.

Dear Mom and Dad,

The greatest single influence in my journey with the Lord has been my family. The Word says, "Honor thy father and thy mother," and it is not difficult to honor those who are honorable. You can demand obedience, but you cannot force children to respect you.

Mom and Dad, you led us by your example. I remember the time I was having a dating problem in college and wrote home asking for some motherly advice. In your reply you said, "I have prayed three things for you ever since you were born— for your salvation, for your calling, and for your life's partner." As I read that letter I remembered one Christmas holiday when we were home from boarding school. I woke up fairly early, about 6:30, and as I walked through the living room I saw your Bible and notebook open on the hearth in front of the fireplace. I stopped and looked at the page open in your notebook, Mom. There was my name, third from the top, after Giles and David. I realized it was your daily prayer list and that you had gotten up early after a long night of typing to have your devotional time and pray for me. As I realized that, a deep peace and assurance filled my heart that God was going to answer your prayers and take care of my situation. And He did. God sent Leigh Ann to be my lovely wife and has blessed us with precious Sarah and Giles.

It was not my choice to be born in a bush hospital in Rhodesia; it was not my choice to leave home and go to boarding school in fourth grade. But I praise our precious Lord that you were both obedient to God's call, trusting God to take care of your children.

When the war raged in Rhodesia, I faced the possibility that you might have to give your lives in God's service. I knew you had always trusted us boys in God's hands and I had to trust Him to do with my parents what would best serve His eternal purpose.

I have spent most of my life in Africa and have a deep love for this land and its people. After I became a Christian in high school, there was a constant and abiding yearning for missions that was the lodestone around which all my training and education took place. As I serve here in Botswana as a church planter and developer, the thing that gives me great courage and strength is the example I saw lived out in your life and the reality of your faith and convictions that was evident in all you did. If I can pass that legacy on to my own children, I will consider my life to have been a success.

I love you. Gordon.

Then there was that rare phone call from David, now a missionary doctor serving in a remote area of Ghana. It was thrilling to talk with him and Laurel. Wana Ann and Giles especially recalled what David had once written.

"Mom and Dad, you know my involvement in missions really began with your involvement in missions. Most of the major steps in the development of my life are in some way a reflection of your own love for, belief in, and commitment to God. My understanding of God as personal, living, compassionate, merciful, seeking, and concerned for an entire world has developed not only from my personal experience with Him, but from your understanding of Him in this way and this expression of Him in your lives.

"While at the Glorieta Foreign Mission Conference I felt that God wanted to use my life in foreign missions as a medical missionary. It was a great advantage to grow up on the missions field because I was not afraid of going to 'deepest, darkest Africa' or any other place I might be sent.

"Much of my Christian growth in recent years has been related to my marriage to Laurel. Mom and Dad, your own commitment to marriage, your love for each other, and your willingness to be considerate of each other's needs was a terrific example to me in the development of my relationship with Laurel.

"I guess what I've realized lately is that I am enormously privileged to have been reared in a home where God is a reality and following Him a way of life. As I work at the hospital on the missions field at Nalerigu, the bold example of Christ and my spiritual elders, together with what

I have witnessed in your lives, continues to be a personal encouragement and challenge. I hope that my children Rachel Ann and Ruth will likewise see Christ in me."

Eldest son Giles was teaching part-time at the Louisiana State University College of Medicine in Baton Rouge, Louisiana, and had a part-time practice in gynecology oncology. He, wife Amy, and their four children, Daniel, Katie, Audrey and Julie, were active members of their church, emphasizing missions both with their service and participation in missions organizations and with their stewardship.

Gregg, wife Donna, and sons Nathan and Stephen, were serving in his beloved Zimbabwe. He truly had become, as the Africans had said many years earlier, a child of the people.

"You know, Wana Ann, Gregg always said that our boys were answered prayers," reminded Giles.

"As we retire 36 years after our appointment, three of them are on the missions field: David as a missionary surgeon in Ghana and Gordon in Botswana and Gregg in Zimbabwe as evangelists and church planters and developers.

"Giles is serving his Lord through his local church, heightening awareness of the importance of missions involvement and support. It's good to have Grady living close to us, now, too. Gregg calls them all the fruits of our faithfulness."

"Well, they are priceless treasures to their mother," whispered Wana Ann.

"I always said we hoped to serve our Master as medical missionaries wherever He led us to go. The work of a doctor on the missions field is the same as it is anywhere else—to heal disease, prevent suffering, usher in life, ease into death, and make and record observations that might add to the science of medicine. The work of a Christian doctor is the same also—to help win souls to Christ through serving the physical needs of people—for to God there are no foreign fields."

"We saw many things during those years and grew to love God's good, perfect, and acceptable will for us. The people were responsive to our medical ministry and to the Gospel message. The evangelistic, educational, and medical work all expanded and grew. Through the years, God used many people to sustain and strengthen us. Perhaps now, He can use us to encourage, motivate, and strengthen others to be involved in missions as we share our experiences with them, starting with that 35th church anniversary celebration," Wana Ann said.

"I remember the call we received," Wana Ann reflected, "not many months after the Sanyati Baptist Hospital opened, to go to one of the villages to help a woman deliver her baby. Giles, you had gone to purchase supplies and I took nurse Emma Gazi with me in the RAF ambulance. Arriving at her *kraal*, we found that the *ambuyas* had been working with her for more than a day. We delivered very small premature twins, the first stillborn, with the second living for only a few moments. Then we took the mother to the hospital where she needed a blood transfusion and other care. While the blood was dripping into her daughter's vein, the mother began to talk to nurse Emma.

"With tears in her eyes, she said, 'Two years ago no doctor and no hospital were here. My older daughter had this same trouble having her baby. Missionary Bowlin tried to take her to town. It was during the rains and the lorry broke down. She and her baby died by the roadside. If the doctors, nurses, and the hospital were not here now, this daughter of mine would be dead, too. How we thank God for sending you to help us.'

"With that woman, I thank God for His love and for His love of His children that sent us there."

Wana Ann and Giles today.

Giles as a young military man in World War II.

Wana Ann receives her medical degree from Baylor.

126

David, Gordon, and Gregg Fort model their school uniforms.

David Fort (*left*) and Jerry Fray try to study at Sanyati, but sometimes it isn't easy!

Wana Ann teaches Gregg at the Baptist school for missionary children.

Giles Fort shares hope with an African man at Sanyati.

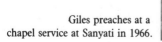

Giles preaches at a chapel service at Sanyati in 1966.

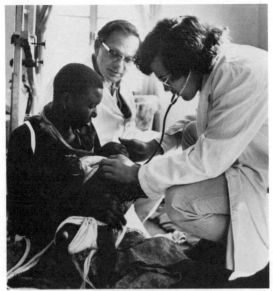

Giles Fort III examines a young patient while his father looks on. Giles, a medical student at the time, was visiting his parents.

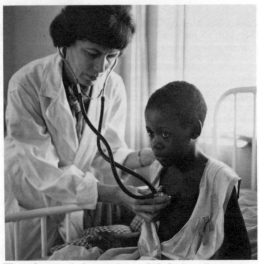

Wana Ann tenderly examines a little heart patient.